Does a Good Soldier have to be a MURDERER?

(Seven Great Swanky Armies of Voluntary Working Soldiers!)

By
The Worldwide People's Revolution!®

Book 027 ★

(A Photo of a Potential Working Soldier. Thank you, Dan.)

Copyright, Dedication and Introduction

By our Selected King's Chief Editor,
Dr. Samuel Walker Edison, Ph.D., MA., BS and QC!

ISBN — 13: 978-1723-5682-82
ISBN — 10: 1723-5682-87

00-01 [_] This Good Book is COPYRIGHTED AD 2018—4019, by **The Worldwide People's Revolution!®**, whose Selected King is the Inspired Author of more than 350 Unique Books, which are getting more and more Popular among Well-Educated People: beCause of the Fact that he has **"Guaranteed Solutions"** (Book 080) for our Massive Problems — such as Unemployment, Low Wages, Poverty, Crimes, Illegal Immigration, Drug Trafficking, Education Slavery, Work Slavery, Tax Slavery, Insurance Slavery, Interest Slavery, Drug Slavery, Sex Slavery, Abortions, Divorces, a False Economy, Unfair Wages, False Prosperity, and Election Deceptions. Indeed, he Offers Freedom with a Capital F, Liberty with a Capital L, and Justice for ALL with a Capital J! Therefore, have some Faith with a Capital F, O Lady Doubtfulness, and Understand that **"All of the Arguments are in Favor of our Selected King, who has Zero Challengers!"** for the Highest Office in the Whole World, as the Elected King of **"The New RIGHTEOUS One-World Government!" (HOW to Establish a Righteous One-World Government without Going to WAR!) By The Worldwide People's Revolution!®**, Book 056. Therefore, **"Before you Attend another Election Deception, you should Carefully Study this Inspired Book with an Honest Open Mind!" By The Worldwide People's Revolution!®**

00-02 [_] All Rights are Reserved for the Non-Federal Burden of Honest Investigators (N-FBI) and the Central Intelligent Agencies (CIA), who are Seeking Provable and Irrefutable Truths: beCause they Understand that only TRUTHS can Liberate us TAX SLAVES from the Unsanitary Prison of Capitalist LIES, whose Chief Proponent presently Resides not far from **"The BIG White OUTHOUSE on the Not-so-Biblical Capitol DUNGHILL!"** (Book 023) in the District of Chief Criminals, in Washington, which Outhouse has the 2 very Odious Holes for the Dimwitcrats and Reprobates to Squat on, which Stinks from the Top to the Bottom with Ancient Elephant Droppings, and Fresh Political Donkey Dung, if you know what I Mean.

00-03 [_] No Portion of this Inspired Book shall be Reproduced by any Means for Sale without Written Permission from **The Worldwide People's Revolution!®** However, with our Permission, anyone and everyone in the Whole World is Welcome to Reproduce Exact Copies, and Sell them for a Reasonable Profit, and KEEP 90 percent of the Net Profits for their own Prosperity, Peace and Happiness: beCause our Selected King only wants 10% of the Net Profits for the Construction of **"The Great World TEMPLE of PEACE!" (The Glory of Jerusalem Arises Again!) By The Worldwide People's Revolution!®** Book 017. Yes, that will be the Headquarters for **"The New RIGHTEOUS One-World Government!"** — which will be the Tallest and Largest Capital Building in the Whole World, which will be Built in 60 Great Stone Terraces, with 10 Minor Terraces within each Great Terrace, being about a Mile High and 8 Miles in Diameter, being Filled with Beautiful Stone Dome Home Complexes for the Elected Officials, who will Live and Work within that Great Temple, which will have no Secret Meetings of the most Intelligent Minds! †§‡

FOUR SCORE AND SEVEN YEARS
AGO OUR FATHERS BROUGHT FORTH
ON THIS CONTINENT A NEW NATION
CONCEIVED IN LIBERTY AND DEDICA-
TED TO THE PROPOSITION THAT ALL
MEN ARE CREATED EQUAL.
NOW WE ARE ENGAGED IN A GREAT
CIVIL WAR TESTING WHETHER THAT
NATION OR ANY NATION SO CON-
CEIVED AND SO DEDICATED CAN LONG
ENDURE. WE ARE MET ON A GREAT
BATTLEFIELD OF THAT WAR. WE HAVE
COME TO DEDICATE A PORTION OF
THAT FIELD AS A FINAL RESTING
PLACE FOR THOSE WHO HERE GAVE
THEIR LIVES THAT THAT NATION
MIGHT LIVE. IT IS ALTOGETHER FIT-
TING AND PROPER THAT WE SHOULD
DO THIS. BUT IN A LARGER SENSE
WE CAN NOT DEDICATE~WE CAN NOT
CONSECRATE~WE CAN NOT HALLOW~
THIS GROUND. THE BRAVE MEN LIV-
ING AND DEAD WHO STRUGGLED HERE
HAVE CONSECRATED IT FAR ABOVE
OUR POOR POWER TO ADD OR DETRACT.
THE WORLD WILL LITTLE NOTE NOR
LONG REMEMBER WHAT WE SAY HERE
BUT IT CAN NEVER FORGET WHAT THEY
DID HERE. IT IS FOR US THE LIVING
RATHER TO BE DEDICATED HERE TO
THE UNFINISHED WORK WHICH THEY
WHO FOUGHT HERE HAVE THUS FAR
SO NOBLY ADVANCED. IT IS RATHER FOR
US TO BE HERE DEDICATED TO THE
GREAT TASK REMAINING BEFORE US~
THAT FROM THESE HONORED DEAD
WE TAKE INCREASED DEVOTION TO
THAT CAUSE FOR WHICH THEY GAVE THE
LAST FULL MEASURE OF DEVOTION~
THAT WE HERE HIGHLY RESOLVE THAT
THESE DEAD SHALL NOT HAVE DIED IN
VAIN~THAT THIS NATION UNDER GOD
SHALL HAVE A NEW BIRTH OF FREEDOM~
AND THAT GOVERNMENT OF THE PEOPLE
BY THE PEOPLE FOR THE PEOPLE SHALL
NOT PERISH FROM THE EARTH.

00-04 [_] Yes, even Abe Lincoln would Agree that we have much Unfinished Work that Needs Doing by **"Seven Great Armies of Working Soldiers!" (HOW to Provide a Way for Everyone to WORK: so as to Eliminate Poverty, Crimes, Drug Abuses, Prisons and Unnecessary Taxes!) By The Worldwide People's Revolution!®**, Book 015, which makes Perfect Sense to the Thinking Person, who can also Remember Well, who is Blest with Common Sense and Good Understanding. We Trust that you are one of those Blest People, who does not have to be Humiliated by some God-given Weakness, just to Confess that Murder is Murder, no matter HOW you go about Doing it, whereby tens of thousands of "War Heroes" have Committed SUICIDE: beCause of having their Consciences Racked with GUILT: beCause of Murdering Innocent People in Hateful Wars, which is not something that Normally Bothers the Dead Consciences of Fighter Pilots, who Drop Bombs from far up in the Sky, who do not get to See nor Smell the Blood and Spilled Guts of their Mutilated Victims, as in the Cases of Fire Bombings during World War 2, when tens of thousands of Japanese and German Cities were FIRE BOMBED by Professing American and British "Christians," who Sincerely Believed that they were doing Almighty God a "Special Service" by Murdering Millions of Innocent Men, Women and Children, who had nothing to do with the War Game, who were no more Guilty of War Crimes than Saint Mary and the Baby Jesus. {See www.Amazon.com for a Free Description and Book Preview of the above Mentioned Book, or any number of other Inspired Books by our Selected King, which are Guaranteed to Satisfy the Belly of your Mind.}

00-05 [_] All Rights on this Book are Reserved for and DEDICATED to the Innocent Victims of Hateful Wars, all of the Way Back to the Time of Moses, who would have Loved all such Inspired Literature as this. {For the Proof of that, see: **"The New MAGNIFIED Version of the Book of DEUTERONOMY!" (The Understandable Version of Deuteronomy in Plain English!) By The Worldwide People's Revolution!®** Book 084.} Therefore, no Portion of this Good Book shall be Reproduced by any Means for Sale without Written Permission from **The Worldwide People's Revolution!®** However, with that Permission, anyone in the World may Reproduce Exact Copies for Sale at a Reasonable Price, and Keep 90% of the Net Profits for their own Financial Gain, even as it states on page 2: beCause our Selected King only wants 10 percent of the Net Profits for the Construction of **the Great World TEMPLE of PEACE**, in Jerusalem, Iran, Syria, Germany, Venezuela, Mexico, or even in the Great State of Flexible Texas, if Israelis are not Interested in it, which will be the Tallest and Largest and Most Beautiful Dodecagon Building in the Whole World, being nearly a Mile Tall and 8 Miles or more in Diameter, being Built Up in 60 Great Stone Dodecagon TERRACES at 33° Angles, each one being about 60 feet Tall, being Crowned with Beautiful and Permanent Arcaded Stone Wind Funnels for Swanky Electric Wind Generators for Producing "Free" Electricity throughout the Great Temple, whereby Amazonian Water from Lower Cisterns will be Pumped Up to Higher Cisterns, in Order to Produce LIVING WATER for everyone who Lives in or Visits that Great Temple of PEACE! †‡

00-06 [_] Indeed, each of the Great Dodecagon Terraces will be about 240 feet Wide at the Top, being Covered with Vegetable Gardens, Vineyards, Orchards, and Flower Gardens Planted in the Terraces, with 6 Lesser Terraces facing the Fronts of each of the Great Terraces, which Lesser Terraces will be about 12 feet Wide at their Tops, with Beautiful Stone Balustrades along the Outer Edges of Granite Walkways, which Border Special Flower Gardens, Vineyards, Berry Bushes, and Dwarf Fruit Trees and Nut Trees along those Walkways, which will Surround the Great Temple, which will be lit up with Special Colored Lights at Night for one Spectacular Night Show by and for **"Seven Great Swanky Armies of Voluntary Working Soldiers!"** and their Invited Guests!

00-07 [_] Moreover, each of those Great Terraces will be Blest with Beautiful Stone Dome Home Complexes under the Terraced Gardens, which will have Agate Windows, Polished Marble Walls, Polished Granite Floors, Ceramic-tiled Bathrooms, Kitchens, Walk-in Coolers, Freezers, and large Cisterns for Water Storage for Waterfalls and Spectacular Water Shows at Night, after which **"The Swanky Association of Professional Musicians"** will suddenly appear with their Trumpets, Violins, Guitars, Drums, Flutes, and other Instruments to Play *"Silent Night, Holy Night,"* or whatever is on their Happy Sweetened Minds! Yes, their First Song may be *The Battle Hymn of the Republic,"* just for Poor Old Abe Lincoln, who will Naturally have to be Raise Up from the Dead, along with Thomas Edison and Frank Lloyd Wright, just to get everything Designed Correctly and Engineered Perfectly, which Beautiful Stone Dome Home Complexes will be Self-air-conditioned, Fireproof, Mouse-proof, Termite-proof, Hail-proof, Tornado-proof, Rot-proof, Paint-proof, Insurances-proof, and TAX-PROOF, where the Elected Officials of **"The New RIGHTEOUS One-World Government"** will Live with their Volunteer Servants, who will Attend to the many Special Rooms that will be Dedicated to each Nation of Wise People, who will have their Special Rooms within the Great Temple, including Museums, Restaurants, Chapels, Libraries, Theaters, Arts, and Special Crafts, whereby it will be the Most Glorious Building in the World, having Specially-Designed Polished Marble Walls at least 12 feet Thick, in Terraces for Permanent Shelves, Cupboards, and Storage Places; with Polished Granite Floors, Sliced and Polished Agate Windows, and tens of thousands of Dodecagon Stone Dome Homes with Barrel-vault Entrances, overlooking the Surrounding Lands of Israel and Jordan, which will have hundreds of Swanky Hotels for Visitors, which will also be Built Up in Great Terraces: so as to have Pleasant 3-Dimentional Views, while taking Advantage of Elevators and Electric Subway Trains, whereby no Automobiles, Vans, Pickups, Trucks, nor Buses will be Needed, nor Wanted. {See www.Amazon.com for: **"The Great World TEMPLE of PEACE!" (The Glory of Jerusalem Arises Again!)**, Book 017, plus: **"The CONSTITUTION for the New RIICHUS One-World GuvernMINT!" (How all Peoples can get True Justice, and Celebrate the Great Year of JUBILEE!)**, Book 016, plus: **"The Right Design for Living!" (A List of Great Advantages for Building Beautiful Planned City States!)**, Book 012, which is a Companion Book of: **"GLORIOUS Swanky Hotels Castles and Fortresses!" (Beautiful Planned City States for WISE Intelligent Well-Educated People with Common Sense and Good Understanding!) By The Worldwide People's Revolution!®** Book 019.}

00-08 [_] This Special Book is now DEDICATED to the Victims of Capitalism, Socialism, Fascism and Communism, who have been Murdered in Hateful Wars, some of whom have Committed Suicide beCause of being Guilt-ridden from Murdering Innocent Victims of Military Aggressions. May they all Rest in Peace, knowing that a Great Day of Profound Judgment is coming, whereby they will not have Died in Vain: beCause of Inspiring this Good Book. ‡

00-09 [_] So, O Doctor Samuel Walker Edison, what are the Boxes [_] for? Moreover, WHY do you Capitalize so many of your Words, and even repeat things that have already been Revealed? Is that not a Literary "Writer's Sin" of some Kind? †§‡

00-10 [_] Well, if you were the Victim of some Hateful War, who got your Legs and/or Arms Blasted Away by some Mine or Cluster Bomb — as was the Case for Millions of Capitalist Victims in Cambodia, Laos, Vietnam, Afghanistan, Iraq, and Pakistan during these "Modern" Times, you might Consider Capitalizing all such very Important Words: beCause of having Special Meanings for you. For Example, if you were Blinded and made Deaf by one of those "Lovely" All-American "Heroic" Cluster Bombs, when you were only 10 Years Old, whereby you had to spend the Remainder of your Life in Darkness and Silence, you might be Inspired to Capitalize LIFE, Darkness, Eyesight, Hearing, and HATE! Yes, you might even Hate it so much as to Wish to Kill the Son of Satan, who made all of that Possible. However, being Blind and Deaf without any Legs, there would not be very much that you could Do about it, huh? Well, of course, you could always Pray to some Imaginary God of Justice, who almost always arrives at the Scene of the Crime a hundred Years too Late; and you could Hope to God that all such Hateful Wars might END; but, behold, they just keep on Coming! Yes, the Republicans are still "Beating the War Drums" for another War in the Middle East: beCause those Glorious All-American Wars are very Profitable for Rich Weapons Manufacturers, Oil Industries, Gas Companies, Vehicle Manufacturers, and Uniform Factories; but, especially for Rich Gangster Banksters, who have Raked in well over 10 Trillion Dollars from those Profitable Wars! Trust me, NONE of their Money went to those Millions of Victims of the Military Industrial Congressional Bankers' False News Drug Cartel COMPLEX, which is Designed to make Rich People Richer, and Poor People Poorer with a Capital P. Therefore, if you Agree with the above Statement, you should put an X in the above Box, like this: [X], which you should not be Ashamed of: beCause, during the Great Day of God's Judgment, when all of the Books are Opened for Judgment, God will say something like this: "I See that you are an Honest Person: beCause you put a Check Mark or X in that Box, which Indicates that you Agree with the Statement, which I also Agree with. Moreover, if you do not Appreciate the Repetitious Tale Feathers of a Colorful Peacock, which makes a Fantastic Tail Feather Display in the Bright Light of Good Understanding, you should Study the Tale Feathers of a White Chicken, which Symbolizes a Spiritual COWARD, who will have no Position within the Holy Kingdom of All that is Good." {See: **"Justifications for Capitalizations!" (WHY our Selected King Defies the School of Fools by Capitalizing LOVE and HATE!) By The Worldwide People's Revolution!®**, Book 049, plus: **"An Amazing Collection of Wit and Wisdom!" (The Marvelous Tale of the Colorful Peacock from Angel Ridge, King's Mountain, Kentucky; and the Strong Rope of Everlasting Hope!) By The Worldwide People's Revolution!®** Book 048.}

00-11 [_] So, O Doctor Sam, what if we only Agree with PART of that Statement in Verse 00-10 — should we still Check the Box with an X?

00-12 [_] Well, you may ~~Cross Out any Words that you might Disagree with~~, in order to make the Statement Read Correctly to you. Or, you may use a Yellow Highlighter to Mark any Words that you Agree with, while also making a Check Mark ☑ or X in the so-called "Box." Moreover, you may Add any Important Words in the Margins, in order to make any Statements read Correctly according to your Honest Viewpoints.

00-13 [_] So, are you saying, O Doctor Sam, that we shall be Judged by the Ridiculous Words within this uninspired book? †§‡

00-14 [_] I Warn you to be Careful HOW you Judge all such Books: beCause it is Clearly Written in *the Book of Revelation* that all of the Good Books shall be Opened during the Day of Judgment, whereby we shall all be Judged, according to whatever has been Written. (See the New MAGNIFIED Version of Chapter 20, Verse 12.)

00-15 [_] O Doctor Sam, what if we do not Believe the New MAGNIFIED Version (NMV) of the *Scriptures*? What if we Live by the King James Authorized Version, only, and Disregard all other Versions — will we still be Judged According to whatever Provable Truths might be Found in the New MAGNIFIED Version, which is nothing more than the Honest Interpretation of some so-called RIGHTEOUS King, whom we have never Met, nor even Heard of? {See: **"The Process of Making a RIGHTEOUS KING!" (A Fascinating Autobiography of our Selected King!) By The Worldwide People's Revolution!®** Book 082.}

00-16 [_] Well, our Potential Friend, it makes no Difference to the Members of **The Worldwide People's Revolution!®**, even if you are an Atheist: beCause we Understand that there are more than 200 Contradictory Versions of that so-called "Holy Bible," which is Proof that all of them must be Mistranslations of the Original Collections of Books, which have never been Discovered: beCause, if there were any one Perfect Version, it would Prove the other Versions to be WRong. However, it is utterly Foolish to Vainly Imagine that ALL Important Truths can be Found within Bibles, which do not even Explain HOW to Plant Fruit Trees Properly, nor how to Nourish them Properly, whereby they might Produce Healthy Sweet Fruits to Eat. Therefore, we are Reliant on many other Books of Important Information, just to Survive in this World of Wonders. So, the Important Thing is to Study Books for whatever Truths that we might Discover within them, even if they come from the Mouth of Balaam's Ass. (See *Numbers 22* in whatever Version you Like.)

Explanations for Symbols that are used within this Book and within all other Literature by The Worldwide People's Revolution!®

† This Dagger is called "the Sword of Controversy," which Means that someone Disagrees with the Statement, which could include the Author, himself, who does not always Agree with his own Statements: beCause he Writes by the Spirit of Inspiration, which is a Gift from God, who does not always Agree with his own Statements, which are followed by …

‡ The Double-edged Sword of Controversies, which Means that all such Statements must be Proven, and all Important Issues must be Settled at: **"The Great Worldwide TELEVISED Court HEARING!" (That Great Meeting of the Most Intelligent and Well-Educated Minds!) By The Worldwide People's Revolution!®** Book 041.

§ This Section Symbol represents Sarcastic Statements, which usually Mean the Opposite of whatever has been Stated. 2 such Symbols, together (§§), Means that it is a Double Sarcasm, which is so Sarcastic that it Proves itself to be WRong. For Example, "No Murderous Soldier wants to become a Moderately Rich Working Soldier: because a Murderous Solder might have to Give Up Murdering, which would make him Sick to his Stomach: beCause he Loves to let Out the Blood and Guts of other Healthy Beautiful Young Men, which Fills his Soul with LOVE and JOY! Yes, his Wife and Children also Love him for his Murders, and can hardly wait to Hear about more of them: beCause they are Spiritually Blinded by their PRIDE, whereby they get up each Morning and Crow Loudly about their Goodness and Greatness, while Pledging their Allegiance to the Bloody Rag of **'The Divided States of United Lies!' (The so-called 'United States of North America' in Disguise!)**, Book 058, which Awards the Best Murderers with Medals of Honor from the Biblical God, who is Represented by the Pure Gold on the Medals." Smile, O Sourpuss! †§‡§§

The Delicious Menu for a Feast of Provable Truths

This Book contains about 45,000 Words and one Photograph.

{FOOTNOTE: This is perhaps the only Book in the World that has 10 Verses in each Chapter, except for the Introduction, all of which Harmonize as just one Chapter: beCause the End of each Chapter Leads into the next Chapter, whereby the Reader is almost Compelled to read the entire Book during one sitting, which is quite possible and most practical to do so. Yes, I recommend it: beCause the Thoughts will not be "Broken Up" by any Distractions — that is, unless you are Surrounded by a Distracting Environment, such as Children Playing Cowboys and Indians on "Stick Horses," TVs Running, Radios Advertising Lies, etc. Therefore, it is also Highly Recommended that you find yourself a Comfortable, Quiet and Peaceful Place to Read this Inspired Book with a Capital R, as in Carefully, Thoughtfully, Prayerfully, and with an Honest Open Mind: beCause this could be the very Book that PREVENTS another Hateful Horrible World War, if its Inspired Words of Provable Truths get into the Minds and Hearts of Enough People, who have always Known, Instinctively, that there must be a Way to Live without Murdering other People, and without them Murdering us, nor even Wanting to Murder us. Yes, it does Require an OUNCE of PREVENTION that is Worth far more than a Pound of Cures, as they say. Therefore, do not Allow yourself, nor anyone else, to Cover Up your Window of Faith with their Dark Curtains of Doubt and Unbelief; but, Draw Back those Dark Curtains, and Allow the Full Light of Lovable Truths to Shine Brightly into the Darkness of your own Ignorance, whereby you can Discover the KEY of the Nolij of ALL that GOOD and EVIL, whereby you can Confess it, and thus Unlock the Door of Confession, and thus Escape from the Hateful Prison of Traditional Lies, into the Paradise of Peace and True Happiness, in the Blest Land of Perfect Oneness, as a WORKING Soldier, who Shares his Labors with other Working Soldiers: so as to Produce that Wonderful Paradise, whereby all of you become Moderately RICH in all Ways! Trust me, you will Better Understand what I am saying by the Time that you Finish Reading this Inspired Book; and then, you will Naturally Want to Read it AGAIN, which is no Sin. In Fact, I have already "Red" it several Times, myself, just to get it Highly Polished and Perfected: beCause I Realize the Great Importance of its Provable Truths, which you will also no doubt Discover — that is, IF you, like "Uneducated Huck Finn" and "Poor Nigger Jim," in *The Adventures of Tom Sawyer,"* by Mark Twain, have the Patience to Persist unto the Fascinating END.}

— Chapter 01 —

What IS a GOOD Soldier?

{Please Check any Boxes with Statements that you Agree with. Thank you.}

01-01 [_] I Sincerely Believe that a Good Soldier is one who Swears to Uphold the Constitution for the United States of America, and Actually Does just Exactly that: beCause it is a Good Document, which was Inspired by some God, and possibly by the Hebrew God, even though it is Missing all of the Necessary Elizabethan English with "thee's," "thou's," "thy's" and "thines," whereby it would be Authentic *Scriptures,* being Inspired by the one and only True God! †§‡

01-02 [_] I Refuse to Check the above Box with an X: beCause, like the Unholy Mutilated *Bible,* the Constitution for the United States is Subject to a thousand Different Interpretations, which is WHY we have a United States Supreme Court, which is made up of 9 Judges (at least most of the Time), who have also Sworn to Uphold the Constitution of the United States: beCause every Member of the Federal Government, including all Military Personnel, must make such an Oath of Allegiance, even as the Elected President does during his Inauguration Day, which is just a Formal Ceremony, which no one Accepts as anything very Serious with a Capital S: beCause no President, Congressperson, nor Supreme Court Judge has ever Actually Upheld the Constitution for **"The Divided States of United Lies," (The so-called "United States of North America" in Disguise!)** during the past 100+ Years, or else Congress would be Minting and Printing American Money, rather than having Gangster Banksters do it for them, who Cheerfully and "Secretly" Collect TRILLIONS of Dollars in Interest Payments on LOANS to the Federal Government, which is Unconstitutional. Indeed, the Constitution does not state that "Bankers shall Coin and Print American Money," but, that CONGRESS shall Coin the Money, and Regulate the Value thereof, which it does NOT Presently DO, which is a "Governmental Sin," you might say, which can be Proven in a Courtroom. †§‡

01-03 [_] I Disagree with you, O Selected King of **The Worldwide People's Revolution!®**: beCause we have what is known as the "Federal Reserve Bank," which is not Actually a *Federal* Bank, at all: beCause it is a PRIVATE Bank, whose Stockholders mostly Reside in Europe, who also get their Fair Share of those Interest Payments on the Loans that the so-called "Federal" Reserve Bank Loans to the Federal Government of **"The Divided States of United Lies!"** Yes, it is called a "Money Game," which is Played by RICH Lying Edomite Bankers, who have made the Monetary System so Complicated that the Average American has no Idea what is even Happening, nor could most Americans care less: beCause they are only Interested in their own Personal Prosperity. Indeed, if they have Money to Spend, they just Ignore whatever is going on in the District of Criminals, in Washington, which is WHY 50% or more of Americans do not even bother themselves to VOTE in the Election Deceptions! After all, what Good does it do to Vote for one of 2 or 3 WRong Political Parties, since they are all "Chewing on Different Corners of the same Old Bloody Rag," as my Daddy used to say. Yes, they are all Working for the Military Industrial Congressional Bankers' False News Media COMPLEX, and they all Know it. However, there is no Way to bring all of those High-ranking Criminals to COURT for Failing to Uphold the

Constitution: beCause, WHO would be Brave Enough to Stand Up to their Army Tanks, like the Young Man did in Tiananmen Square, in Beijing, China, and DEMAND Justice with a Capital J? Indeed, such a Person would be Fighting Against the entire Evil Capitalist Empire, which is Based on a False Foundation of Outlandish LIES — such as the Goodness of Election Deceptions! †§‡ {See www.Amazon.com for: **"The BIG White OUTHOUSE on the Not-so-Biblical Capitol DUNGHILL!" (The Chief Sins of the Divided States of United Lies!)**, Book 023, plus: **"The UGLY Scarred Dishonest Face of Poor Old Miserable UNCLE SAM!" (A Memorial Day Legacy!) By The Worldwide People's Revolution!®**, Book 054, which is a Companion Book of: **"Are we Tax Slaves of a Lower Order than those Lying EDOMITES?" (HOW to be Liberated from all Slavery, Worldwide!) By The Worldwide People's Revolution!®** Book 052.}

01-04 [_] So, what are the little Daggers (†‡) for, O Selected King?

01-05 [_] Well, a Single Sword (†) is called "The Sword of Controversy," which Means that someone Disagrees with the Statement. Perhaps a "Facts Check" is necessary to Correct the Statement. Whatever the Case, not everything within such Statements is 100% Reliable. For Example, in Verse 01-03, it reads: "... whose Stockholders mostly Reside in Europe," which I have "Heard" is the Case; but, I have not Proven it to be True, nor would I have any Idea just Exactly HOW to go about Proving it, since that is not my "Field of Expertise," you might say. However, I am almost Certain that someone knows just Exactly HOW to Check it out and Prove it in a Courtroom, which is WHY the above Statement in Verse 01-03 is followed by "The Double-edged Sword of Controversy," (‡) which Means that all such Statements should be brought to the Attention of **"The Great Worldwide TELEVISED Court HEARING,"** whereby such Statements can be Proven in that Special Courtroom, and thus the Controversies about the so-called "Federal" Reserve Bank can be "Laid to Rest" in "The Little-remembered Unpleasant Valley Slimmetery (Cemetery for Skeletons)," whereby that Subject will not have to be Raised Again from the Dead, you might say: beCause that Issue will be Settled, once and for all Time, and thus be Laid to Rest, along with a LOT of other Suspected Subjects — such as, WHO Actually Assassinated President Kennedy? Were 6 Million Jews Murdered in the Holocaust during World War 2? Did Men Land on the Moon, and Escape from it without a Rocket Launcher nor X-amount of Rocket Fuel, whereby they Supposedly "Jettisoned" away from the Moon at about 4,000 MpH? Were EXPLOSIVES used in the Destruction of World Trade Center (WTC) Tower 7 during September 11th, 2001, and so on?! However, I am Sure that X-amount of Rich Hogs will not Love any such Court Hearings, and will be Grunting Against the Idea as soon as they Hear about it. After all, the "Federal Reserve Bank" is not a Reserve of any Kind: beCause **"The Divided States of United Lies"** is more than 147 TRILLION Dollars in Debt to Rich Bankers and Money Lenders, including National Debts, State Debts, County Debts, City Debts, Business Debts, College Loan Debts, Personal Debts, and Obligatory Debts — such as Future Social Security Payments, which will Add Up to an Astounding Figure within the next 100 Years, which none of our Forefathers could have ever Imagined, or else they might have Re-written their Constitution, whereby those Lying Zionist Edomite Gangster Banksters would have been OUTLAWED! Indeed, without their "Services," us Americans would have LOTS of Money, even as God, himself, Proved in my Inspired Book, called: **"God Speaks and Whole World Listens!" (Fire on the Mountain from the Burning Bush by the Spirit of Truth!)**, Book 026. Yes, no Honest Person can Rightly Deny that Fact of Life, even if he or she is Suffering with Chronic Constipation of the Mind! †§‡

01-06 [_] I Disagree with you, O Selected King of **The Worldwide People's Revolution!®**: beCause I am an Honest Person, and I Deny that so-called "Fact of Life," which is Based on the Presumption that Rich Bankers are in Control of this World of Woes, when it is Actually Rich Drug Companies, Insurance Agencies, and Weapons Manufacturers that are in Control, which is WHY we must have those "Eternal Wars," just to keep those Edomites Happy. †§‡ See B-052, which is far more Powerful than all Atomic and Hydrogen Bombs, combined, O Peabrain Peacock!

01-07 [_] So, what is the little Squiggly Mark (§) for?

01-08 [_] Well, that Section Mark (§) is used throughout my Inspired Books to Symbolize a Sarcasm, while 2 such Marks (§§), together, Symbolize a DOUBLE Sarcasm, which is so Sarcastic that the Statement Proves itself to be WRong. For Example, there are no Corrupted Politicians in Washington, District of Corruptions, which Explains WHY they are all Notorious for their Christian Good Deeds — such as Dropping 50 Million Tons of Bombs on LAOS and CAMBODIA, during 1969, without even Declaring War on them! †§‡§§ {FOOTNOTE: See Howard Zinn's book, called: **"A People's History of the United States,"** which Lists at least a hundred similar Atrocities, for which no one has given an Account in any Courtroom! In other Words, when **"The Divided States of United Lies"** commits some War Crime, it is Okay with the United States Supreme Court, who have also Sworn to Uphold the Constitution, which is Wrapped in Velvet and Sealed with Golden Stickers, which no one should Touch: beCause that Constitution is a "Sacred Thing," right next to that "Holy Bible," which no one should Dare to ALTER by any Means, lest the little Children might come to Understand the TRUTH, the Whole Truth, and nothing but the Truth! Indeed, not even Howard Zinn Understood most of the Bible Prophecies: beCause of their VAGUENESS, whereby he Avoided all such *Scriptures,* which are about as Clear as MUD. For Example, *"Prove all Provable Things, and Cling Tightly to ALL that is GOOD,"* which would Naturally Include the Good Drugs and Bad Foods Administration, which Authorized the Use of DDT, for Decades, plus Cancer-Causing ROUNDUP, and no less than 30,000 other Poisonous and Harmful Chemicals in our Foods and Drinks: beCause it was Profitable for those Lying Conniving EDOMITES! Yes, they have Gained TRILLIONS of Dollars by the Approvals of those Edomites, who should be Brought to COURT in Chains and Shackles, if they do not Willingly Submit to **"The Swanky Sword of Divine Truths!" (The Most Powerful Weapon in the Whole Universe!) By The Worldwide People's Revolution!® Book 067.** †§‡}

01-09 [_] So, O Elected King of **The Worldwide People's Revolution!®**, just Exactly what IS a GOOD Soldier?

01-10 [_] Well, that is someone who Loves and Cheerfully Obeys his or her Commanding Officer, who must be Honest, Nolijuboul, Well-Educated, Trustworthy, Morally Straight, Respectable, Responsible, Self-disciplined, Fair, Just, Compassionate, Understanding, True to his Words, and BRAVE! Yes, General Robert E. Lee was just such a Person, for which one of his Soldiers said: "I would Follow that Old Man into Hellfire, if he asked me to." And thus he did, and the Devil was Laughing at him the whole Time: beCause Robert E. was being Overly Zealous for an Unjust Cause, which Issue should have been Settled in a Courtroom, as Robert Educated Lee BEGGED them to Do, even in the CONgress of **"The Divided States of United Lies!"** and not in any Bloody Gory Hateful WAR, whereby some half-million Young Men Died for NOTHING, while Millions more Suffered Horrible Wounds, and often Hobbled around with Crutches, until they Died with Disgusting PRIDE! †§‡

— Chapter 02 —

What is a BRAVE Soldier?

02-01 [_] So, O Selected King of **The Worldwide People's Revolution!®**, are you not Afraid of being too Brave? After all, when you are Boldly Standing Up to Rich Bankers, Rich Drug Pushers, Rich Industrialists, Rich Insurance Agencies, Rich Oil Companies, Rich Gas Companies, Rich Car Manufacturers, Rich Chemical Corporations, and an entire List of Rich HOGS with Big Teeth — including those Grunting Rich Political HOGS in Washington, whose Chief Liar squats on a Gold-plated Toilet — you are putting yourself in a more Dangerous Position than David put himself in when he Faced Goliath and his 4 Giant Brothers. Yes, your Story is another David and Goliath Story: beCause you are Confronting the Giant Industries of the World, beginning with those Hateful Lying Zionist Edomite Bankers of the Bernie Madoff and Judas Iscariot Club, who have Wittingly Collected TRILLIONS of Dollars for doing almost nothing, while Billions of People have Suffered in their Indebted States of EXTREME Poverty for a Lack of Money. Indeed, it is Estimated that there are Presently more than a Billion Poor Indians, in India, who Live Below the Imaginary "Poverty Line," whereby they do not even have the Basic Necessities of Life — such as Fresh Clean Air, Pure Running Living Water, Good Wholesome Natural Foods, Proper Natural Clothing, Secure Houses, nor Life Insurance, which does not Cover Suicides. †§‡

02-02 [_] Well, I suppose that you know that India is the largest Democratic Capitalistic Society in the World, which can Rightfully Brag about having more Beggars on their Streets than any other Nation, whereby they can be very PROUD, even as the 400,000+ Americans who Live in Sewage Systems, Culverts, Subways, under Bridges, in Vans, Old Rusty Cars, Pickup Campers, used Recreational Vehicles (RV's) and in Abandoned Houses without Heating nor Cooling Systems! After all, it is said that the Definition of "Insanity" is when you Repeatedly do the same Things, over and over, while Expecting a Different Result. For Example, Americans have been Voting for the Right-WRong / Rong-Riit Parties for Centuries, while Hoping to get Good Results from it. Meanwhile, everything is getting Worse and WORSE, and the Common People are more and more in Debt to those Friendly New York City Bankers: beCAUSE they are the Unholy Ones who Arranged the Rules of the Money Games, whereby they and their Rich Friends around the World, are the only ones who Win, while the Masses of People Struggle to Earn a Living, when there is Technically no Good Reason for anyone to have to Struggle, which I have already Proven in many Good Books. However, just in case this is the First Book of mine that you have "red," I must Repeat a certain Amount of Information, whereby you can also come to Understand that no Bankers were ever Needed, and that all Bankers can be done Away with, whereby we will all be much MUCH Richer! However, you have to be Brave Enough to Study all such Information, and not Fear that it might somehow Cause your Brains to Leak Out of your Head when you Blow your Nose. Indeed, you must Remember that it is not Wise to Judge any Subject, until AFTER you have Learned ALL of the Evidences. Yes, you are Welcome to be the Judge and the Jury in this Case, and Decide for yourself whether or not I am RIIT or WRong, SAAN or Insane, GOUD or Evil. Yes, you are Welcome to Prove it, in a Courtroom, with Law and Order, with or without any Bibles, just as long as you have a RIICHUS JUJ in Charge of it, who Knows his own Bible, who is Perfectly Honest, and is Willing to Confess the Whole Truth when he Learns it. ‡

02-03 [_] So, O Selected King, why are you spelling some of your words in "Funetik Ingglish"? Do you actually Expect us to be Able to "REED and RIIT" all such Words?

02-04 [_] Well, I just Naturally Expect you to have more Intelligence than any of those Political Rabbits in Washington, who come Out of their Stinking Holes every few Years, and Hop all around the Country, to give their Repetitious Political Speeches, until some Overfed Dog with a Long Tongue Barks at them, who cannot even Agree that it would be Wise of us to Spell our Words Consistently, having one or 2 Letters to Represent a single Sound. For Example, there are more than 20 Different Ways to spell the single Sound of "OO," as in: Sch**oo**l, d**o**, r**u**le, thr**ough**, cr**ew**, bl**ue**, fr**ui**t, sh**oe**, man**eu**ver, rendezv**ous**, rh**u**barb, rh**eu**matism, S**iou**x, L**ou**isiana, prosci**u**tto, l**ieu**, gh**ou**l, tw**o**, and p**oo**h! {See www.Amazon.com for: **"The Public School of IGNERUNT FQLZ!" (How we have been GRAATLEE DISEEVD by Capitalism!)**, Book 024, plus: **"The BIG White OUTHOUSE on the Not-so-Biblical Capitol DUNGHILL!" (The Chief Sins of the Divided States of United Lies!) By The Worldwide People's Revolution!® Book 023.}**

02-05 [_] So, O Elected King, are you saying that we Americans are mostly Barbarians, just beCause we have not Learned HOW to Spell our Words According to some Consistent RULES, whereby one Sound is Represented by one or 2 Letters? For Example, a single "Q" is the Vowel Sound in the above Listed Words in Verse 02-04. Therefore, those words would read like this: Skql, dq, rql, thrq, krq, blq, frqt, shq, munqver, rondaavq, rqbrrb, rqmutizm, Sq, Lqeezeeanu, prooshqtoo, lq, gql, 2 and pq.

02-06 [_] Well, very few Americans would be Willing to Confess that they are "Barbarians" of any Kind or Color; but, in the Eyes of the Gods, I am Sure that they are Barbarians, which Naturally Includes myself, in spite of being Able to "Spel evree Werd in thee Ingglish Langgwij, Perfiktlee." {See the above Link for: **"In thu Beeginingz uv Thingz!" (Thu Kreeaashun Stooree frum thu Beegining!)**, Book 025, plus: **"Thu Nq MAGNUFIID Verzhun uv Thu PROVERBZ uv King Solumun in Plaan Ingglish!" (The Understandable Version of the Famous Proverbs of King Solomon in Plain English!) By The Worldwide People's Revolution!® Book 028.}**

02-07 [_] I must Confess one thing, O Elected King, and that is the Fact that you are very Brave to Challenge so many Vain Traditions of Foolish Americans, who just Naturally Seek to Justify almost all of our Evil Ways and Vain Traditions, whereby little Children are FORCED to Learn HOW to Spell their Words in 300+ Inconsistent Ways. For Example, rather than Spell 30 Sounds in 30 Consistent Ways, we are now Spelling them in 300+ Different Ways for the Sake of Confusion, which Prevents many Children from even Learning HOW to "Reed and Riit," whereby they do not even get Interested in Reading nor Writing. Therefore, it seems that Public Schools were Established for the Sole Purpose of Discouraging Children from Learning any Truths, in Order to make them and their Children into Future Education Slaves, Work Slaves, Tax Slaves, Interest Slaves, Insurance Slaves, Drug Slaves, Rent Slaves, Mortgage Bills Slaves, Credit Card Debt Slaves, Heating and Cooling Bills Slaves, Gas Slaves, Water Bills Slaves, Telephone Bills Slaves, Entertainment Bills Slaves, Repair Bills Slaves, Transportation Bills Slaves, Internet Bills Slaves, Sex Slaves, Childcare Slaves, and Endless BILLS SLAVES, huh?

02-08 [_] Well, in some Ways, it might be Better for us that all such Children do not Learn how to do much Writing, lest the World should be Filled with Countless books, which are full of Pure Nonsense, with no **"Guaranteed Solutions"** for anything (See Book 080 in the Long List of other

Fascinating Literature by the same Inspired Author, at the Rear End of this Book.) After all, if a Billion People should write 350+ books, each, that would Amount to more than 350 Billion books, or enough to Fill Noah's Ark several Times, which would be far too many books for God to Open Up during his Great Day of Profound Judgments, much less read aloud each word of each book in less than 10,000 Noah Lifetimes. Therefore, in order for *Revelation 20:12—15* to be True, it would have to read more like this: *"And I saw the Dead People Arise, both Rich and Poor, both Small and Great, both Important and not so Important People, who Stood in front of God, who is the Supreme Judge; and all of the Good Books were Opened Up, including the Book of Life, which contains the Names of all of the People who have not Committed the Unpardonable Sin, which is Blasphemy against the Holy Spirit, who Inspires all Words of Provable Truths, even if they come from the Mouth of Balaam's Ass, including these Words; and the Dead People were Judged According to those Things that were Written in the Good Books, According to their Words and Works, According to their Nolij concerning both Good and Evil: because there is no other Way to Judge them Fairly. Therefore, the Seas gave up those Souls who had Died in the Seas, or who were Buried in the Seas by any Means; and the Graves gave up those Bodies who had been Buried in them, whereby their Flesh was Restored to their Bones, even if they were nothing but Scattered Ashes: beCause of the Power of the Resurrection; and the Angels of Death and Hell gave up the Spirits that had been Committed to them, whereby all such Souls were Judged According to their Words and Works, whereby they were Justified or Condemned. However, being Ignorant concerning the Master Plan of the Master Farmer, none of them could Rightly be Condemned with Satan, the Devil: beCause they were only Deceived by him, whereby the Angels of Death and Hell were Cast into the Lake of Fire, along with Satan and his Multitude of Demon Spirits: beCause they were found Worthy of it, along with whomever Seeks to Justify Lies and Evil Things, whereby they might be Condemned: because no Liar, Deceiver, Fraud, Rapist, Fornicator, Adulterer, Sodomite, Whoremonger, Warmonger, Mutilator, Torturer, Money-monger, Covetous Person, Thief, nor Murderer shall have any Inheritance in the Holy Kingdom of All that is Good. Therefore, whosoever did not have his nor her Name Written in the Book of Life was also Cast Alive into the Lake of Fire with the Beast, the Anti-Christs, the False Prophets, and their Evil Stepfather, the Devil, who Deceives all of the Wicked Nations with the Abundance of his Drugs."* — The New *MAGNIFIED (NMV) Version in Plain English.* †‡ (See *First John 2:18.*)

02-09 [_] So, O Elected King of the Highest Mountains of Good Understanding, it appears to me like you have Bravely ADDED a lot of LIES to the Word of God, which is ONE Word, which is JESUS! †§‡§§ {See: **"The New MAGNIFIED Version of the GOOD NEWS According to Saint JOHN!" (The Gospel According to Saint John Zebedee Boanerges in Plain English) By The Worldwide People's Revolution!® Book 062.**}

02-10 [_] Well, my Potential Honest and Trustworthy Friend, it appears to me that you are Falsely Accusing me of something that I did not Do, since I only Quoted to you the Inspired Words of Provable Truths from another Book, which you did not Prove to be WRong by any Means. Therefore, be Aware of the Evil Spirit that Possesses you: beCause you might also be Cast Alive into that same Lake of Fire and Stinking Sulfur with the Ancient Scribes and Perverted Pharisees — at least Temporarily, if not Permanently — who Rejected any Truths that were not already Found within their Mutilated *Scriptures:* beCause they were Rejecters of Provable Truths, which Condemned them! †§‡ {See *John 3:19—21, KJV,* and Believe it: beCause it is the Truth. See: **"All of the Arguments are in Favor of our Selected King, who has Zero Challengers!"** Book 085.}

— Chapter 03 —

Should a Good Soldier Tell Lies?

03-01 [_] A Good Soldier should NOT Tell any Lies. {Did you Check the Box, my Friend?}

03-02 [_] A Good Soldier MUST Tell Lies: beCause he has Sworn to Uphold the Constitution for the United States of America, AND OBEY HIS SUPERIOR OFFICERS. Therefore, if they ask him to Tell Lies, he must Tell Lies, just to be a Good Soldier. Moreover, if they ask him to Murder some Innocent Soul, then he must Obey, just to be a Good Soldier. †§‡§§

03-03 [_] I am Confused by the Facts. I have no Idea which Box that I should Check with an X.

03-04 [_] Well, if that is True, did you Check the Box for Verse 03-03?

03-05 [_] I am not Honest Enough to Check that Box. However, I will Check this Box.

03-06 [_] Such a Person is Insane. A Good Soldier should NOT Tell any Lies: beCause Lies are NOT GOOD. God does NOT Lie. Murder is BAD. †§‡ (See *First Samuel 15:3, Gay King James Version.*)

03-07 [_] How could a Person Swear to Uphold the Constitution for the United States of America, without Telling any Lies, unless he or she Intended to Overthrow the Federal Government, in Order to Establish **"The New RIGHTEOUS One-World Government!" (HOW to Establish a Righteous One-World Government without Going to WAR!) By The Worldwide People's Revolution!®**, Book 056, which simply Mints and Prints the Necessary New Money with New Faces and Numbers — NOT to Give it Away to Ignorant Idiots, nor to Waste it on Edomite Bankers; but, in Order to Use that New Money WISELY, in Order to HIRE **Seven Great Swanky Armies of Voluntary Working Soldiers**, in Order that they might Help each other to Build those **"GLORIOUS Swanky Hotels Castles and Fortresses!" (Beautiful Planned City States for WISE Intelligent Well-Educated People with Common Sense and Good Understanding!) By The Worldwide People's Revolution!®**, Book 019? Yes, that Stonework will Represent that New Money, which will have to be Earned by Honest Labor, which will make it GOOD Money, and the Best Money in all of this World: beCause it will be Represented by Things of True Value, while our present money is not. Indeed, our present money is represented by the Trash in the Trash Dump, the old Junk Cars in the Junkyard, and the almost Worthless Wooden / Plastic Firetrap Mouse-infested Cockroach Dens, which Ignorant Fools call "American DREAM HOMES," which are Designed to come to Ruin by one Means or another, which Cost ten times more than Proper Houses! Yes, just the Heating and Cooling Bills, Insurance, Interest on Loans, and Property Taxes, alone, make them Unaffordable to at least half of Americans, who have no Desire to make Work Slaves, Interest Slaves, Tax Slaves, nor Insurance Slaves of themselves, just to have Roofs over their Heads, when it is much Better to Live in Mexico, where none of those Evil Things are Needed: beCause the People are Wiser, who Build Small Concrete Houses, which are Fireproof,

Mouse-proof, Hail-proof, Tornado-proof, Termite-proof, Rot-proof, Paint-proof, Self-air-conditioned, Insurance-proof, and Tax-proof: beCause Mexicans are much Smarter than Americans by at least 10 Times! †§‡ {See: **"LIGHTNING STRIKES Versus Lightning Bugs!" (HOW you can Become Moderately RICH, without Telling any Lies nor Selling any Trash!) By The Worldwide People's Revolution!®**, Book 074, which contains more than 60 Enlightening Photographs with Explanations that will Astound you; plus: **"Mexicans are more Intelligent than Americans!" (A Unique Challenge to all Americans and Mexicans!) By The Worldwide People's Revolution!®**, Book 081, plus: **"Are Americans the Most STUPID People who ever Lived?" (HOW Working People can PROSPER and Live in PEACE Under the Rulership of a RIGHTEOUS KING!) By The Worldwide People's Revolution!®** Book 047.}

03-08 [_] A Good Soldier would have to have a Good Government with a Good Constitution, in Order for someone to be a Good Honest Soldier. After all, Wars Require Soldiers to be Deceivers, Thieves, Liars, Murderers, Hypocrites, and whatever is Necessary for Winning the War. †§‡ {See: **"The CONSTITUTION for the New RIGHTEOUS One-World GovernMINT!" (HOW all Peoples can get True Justice, and Celebrate the Great Year of JUBILEE!) By The Worldwide People's Revolution!®** Book 016.}

03-09 [_] I was Raised Up to be an Honest Person at all Times: beCause a Person cannot be Respected nor Loved without Honesty; but, when I got into the Army, I had to Trash my Moral Principles, and make myself a Murderer of Innocent People. Therefore, I Expect that God will also Condemn me during the Judgment Day: beCause "God" is "All that is Good," and Murder is Certainly NOT Good. {See: **"The Seven Basic Spiritual Building Blocks of LIFE!" (Faith Hope Trust Love Patience Persistence and Obedience!) By The Worldwide People's Revolution!®** Book 036.}

03-10 [_] If "God" is "All that is Good," how come he Ordains Wicked People like Saint Joseph Stalin, who had more than 50,000,000 White Christian Russians put to Death during his Reign of Terror in the Union of Soviet Socialist Republicans (USSR), and also Caused the Deaths of more than 40 Million Young Men during World War 2, by not Cheerfully Surrendering to Adolf Hitler, whom God Ordained to Correct those Wicked Jews of the Bernie Madoff and Judas Iscariot Club? Indeed, have you not Studied *Romans 13,* which clearly states that God Ordains the Leaders of ALL Nations, including Germany, Japan, Korea, North Vietnam, Afghanistan, Iraq, Iran, and Pakistan: beCause he is INSANE!? In Fact, that same Insane Chapter was used to Rip the so-called "Illegal Immigrant" Children out of the Arms of their Heart-broken Fathers and Mothers at the Mexican-American Border, in Order to OBEY the Orders of President Donald Lying Hypocrite Jaywalking Trumpeter, who Abused the Minds and Scarred the Hearts of those Poor Little Children and their Homeless Parents, for LIFE, which was a Great EVIL in the Eyes of the Gods, none of whom would have ever Commanded any Leaders to ever Do any such WICKED Things, except for Allah and Jehovah. In Fact, not even Adolf Hitler and his Associates ever did any such Evil Things, except to Separate the Children from the Adults at the Concentration Work Camps, when they Arrived on the Trains, whereby they might all take Showers Separately, and put on Clean Clothes, New Shoes and New Eyeglasses, after they were Deloused; and then they were Reunited with their Families, except for the ones who were Starved to Death after American and British Bombers BOMBED the Railroad Tracks and Bridges that brought the Trainloads of Foods to the NOT-so-NAZI Concentration Camps, about 6 Months before the End of World War 2, for which they Blamed the Losers of the War, and Branded Adolf as the Worst Person who ever Lived!

†§‡§§ {See www.Amazon.com for: **"God Speaks and the Whole World Listens!" (Fire on the Mountain from the Burning Bush by the Spirit of Truth!) By The Worldwide People's Revolution!®**, Book 026, which Explains *Romans 13*. See also: **"For the Love of Money!" (The Strange Things that People Say and Do to Get more Money!) By The Worldwide People's Revolution!®**, Book 003, which Explains what Caused the so-called "Holocaust," which some People have called the HoloHOAX: beCause there is a Mountain of Evidences to Prove that 6 Million Bodies could not be Cremated in a dozen Nazi Ovens within less than 625 Years: beCause it Requires no less than one Hour just to Heat Up the Oven, and then 4 to 12 Hours to Cremate the Body, depending on the Size, Age, Weight, and Density of the Bones; and then another Hour to Cool Off the Oven before the Door could be Safely Opened, lest someone's Eyeballs should be Melted at 4000 °F! Therefore, the Promoters of Edomite LIES must be brought to COURT, and be put to Open Shame for their Propagandist Lies and Insidious Slanders against the German People, who have been making Unjust Reparation Payments in the hundreds of Billions of Dollars to the Jews, ever since World War 2, which was the Fault of the Leaders of the United States, Great Britain and France: beCause, long before the War ever began, Adolf Hitler BEGGED those Allied Leaders to Join him in a Worldwide Radio DEBATE, whereby he might Prove to them that Capitalism is a FALSE Economic System, for which he had the PROOF: beCause Germany had the Best Economy in the World, just 3 Years after Hitler got himself into Power, in 1933, whereby there was ZERO Unemployment in Germany, and TOP WAGES for all Workers, whereby all of the Germans LOVED that Wicked WICKED Adolf Hitler, and so much so that he Rode in OPEN Cars in Public Streets for 8 Years, without anyone Attempting to Assassinate him; but, the Cheering Crowds Greeted him with Millions of Bouquets of Flowers: beCause he Saved them from the Edomite Thing called *the Great Depressions,* which they brought about by Withholding Much-Needed Money from the Little Bankers, who had no Money to Loan to the Education Slaves, Work Slaves, Insurance Slaves, Interest Slaves, Rent Slaves, nor Endless Bills SLAVES — many of whom Lost their Houses, their Farms, their Ranches, their Vehicles, their Furniture, and almost EVERYTHING, except for the Worn-out Rags on their Backs and Butts — Thanks to those Lying Conniving EDOMITES, who Suddenly, within a couple Weeks, came up with hundreds of Billions of Dollars for the Production of Millions of Airplanes, Army Tanks, War Ships, Aircraft Carriers, Submarines, Trucks, Tractors, Trains, Troop Carriers, Jeeps, Countless Bombs, Rifles, Pistols, Bullets, Grenades, Mortars, Land Mines, Tents, Telephones, Uniforms, Sleeping Bags, Cots, Mess Kits, K-rations, Tools and Equipment for going to WAR! So, you might be Wondering WHERE those Edomites got those Trillions of Dollars for making War, after being Penniless just 2 Weeks previously? Well, as usual, they got the Money from their Printing Presses, whereby they Loaned the Money to the Federal Government, whereby they Collected hundreds of Billions of Dollars for USURY — for Interest on their Loans, while their Edomite Friends Collected Billions of Dollars for the Production of those War Machines, Propagandist Movies, and Advertisements for more Soldiers, which almost no one Objected to: beCause the Great Depression was OVER, and the Soldiers were getting Paid Minimum Wages of about 48 dollars per Month for their "Patriotic Services," which most of them sent Home to Help their Extremely Poor and Depressed Parents — none of whom Questioned the Sincerity of their CONgressmen, who Totally Forgot about Article 8 in their Constitution: beCause they were so HAPPY with the War Games! Yes, their Minds and Times were Totally Consumed by the Distractions of WARS, and so much so that not ONE of them ever Reported what I have just now Reported to YOU, O Lover of the Whole Truth — except that this is NOT the *Whole* Truth, which can only be Properly Discovered at: **"The Great Worldwide TELEVISED Court HEARING!" (That Great Meeting of the Most Intelligent**

and Well-Educated Minds!) By The Worldwide People's Revolution!® Book 041. Yes, it is all Documented on YouTube Videos for anyone who has the Spiritual Fortitude to Search for it. You could begin with HoloHOAX and Related Videos — such as www.AE911TRUTH.org which has a Special Video called: **Experts Speak Out,** which the Federal Government just Ignores, while Referring to those 3,000+ Architects and Engineers as "Conspiracy Theorists," who have TONS of Scientific Evidence to Prove that it was a Government False Flag Operation! Meanwhile, those Blabbermouth Politicians make no Mention of it, nor Call for an Unbiased and Thorough Scientific Investigation of those Evil Events: beCause they are in Love with those Lying Conniving Edomites! Otherwise, they would be the First to be Demanding that Great Meeting of the Most Intelligent Minds, which would Include those Architects and Engineers, as well as Dr. Judy Wood, who Observed Things that most People Ignore. *"Seek, and you shall Find,"* as Jesus said. †§‡}

— Chapter 04 —

Good Soldiers are not Driven Insane!

04-01 [_] I must Confess that I am about to be Driven Insane by your Inspired Words of Provable Truths, O Selected King. Indeed, it now seems that almost all of those American "War Heroes" have made Liars of themselves, just by Swearing to Uphold the Constitution for the United States of America, which none of them could Do, even if they Wanted to: because they would have to Overthrow the Evil Capitalist Empire, just to Obey the Constitution, which should have Specifically Stated just Exactly WHO should Mint and Print the Money, and Exactly what that Money should be Used for: so as to not Produce a few Rich Hogs, while at the same Time Producing Hordes of Poor Miserable People. After all, there is no Shortage of Mountains of Rocks in this World of Wonders, whereby we can Build those **GLORIOUS Swanky Hotels Castles and Fortresses,** whereby we can all become Moderately Rich within **"Beautiful Swanky PALACES!" (A New Concept in Living Habits — Swanky Palaces for Poor People!) By The Worldwide People's Revolution!®** Book 066. {See www.Amazon.com for: **"LIGHTNING Versus the Lightning Bug!" (How almost Everyone can become Moderately RICH, without Telling Any Lies nor Selling Any Trash!) By The Worldwide People's Revolution!®,** Book 001, which contains a Special Chapter, called: **"WHO QUALIFIES to Rule Over US?"**}

04-02 [_] I must Confess that I am Extremely Ignorant, whereby none of the above Words make any Sense to me.

04-03 [_] Are you too Ashamed to Ask someone to Help you to Understand them? If so, Stop being Ashamed: beCause, in some Ways, we are all Extremely Ignorant, including so-called "educated" People, who do not even Capitalize such Important Words as Light, Love, Nolij, Truths, Wisdom, Freedom, nor Justice, which is Understandable: beCause they are Prisoners of Society, or Prisoners of Civilizations, which are not so Civilized as they might Imagine: beCause they are still Committing Major Crimes, including the Murders of Innocent People, which is NOT Good. Indeed, it could easily Drive Young Men INSANE: beCause they still have Living

Consciences, and Know within themselves that it is not Right to Murder Innocent People, no matter HOW it is Done. Indeed, it might be less Painful in the Brains to Drop 2,000-pound Bombs from 20,000-feet up in the Sky, than to Butcher someone with a Bayonet; but, the End Results is still the same during the Day of Judgment, when all such Murderers will have to give an Account for it. Guaranteed! ‡

04-04 [_] So, O Elected King, just Exactly HOW can a Drafted Soldier Avoid having a Bad Conscience for being in some Army of Murderers, who are Trained to Murder other Young Men, who also have no Desire to be Murderers?

04-05 [_] Well, he or she can simply Join one of my Seven Great Swanky Armies of Voluntary WORKING Soldiers, whereby it will not be Necessary to Shed Blood: beCause of Constructing Beautiful Planned City States, which are Designed for Defense. {See: **"Seven Great Armies of Working Soldiers!" (HOW to Provide a Way for Everyone to WORK: so as to Eliminate Poverty, Crimes, Drug Abuses, Prisons and Unnecessary Taxes!), Book 015, plus: "The Swanky Associations of Working Soldiers!" (A Fascinating Collection of Various Kinds of Voluntary Working Soldiers!) By The Worldwide People's Revolution!® Book 018.**}

04-06 [_] So, O Elected King, are you Suggesting that we should Abandon our Present Cities of Confusion, and Build **GLORIOUS Swanky Hotels Castles and FORTRESSES,** which no Enemy can Overcome: beCause they are Designed for Total Protection from all Enemies, including the Devil, himself? And just HOW could that be Done, seeing that Satan is everywhere, even Behind Closed Doors in Synagogues, or SINagogues?

04-07 [_] Are you saying that you have Invited Satan into your own House? And, if so, WHY?

04-08 [_] Well, when we brought that Television Home, we most Certainly Invited Satan into our own Living Room: beCause it is Loaded with Temptations and Advertisements for Drugs and all Kinds of Junk that we could Live Happily without. Ask the Wild Mountain Goats, if you Doubt it. Indeed, they seem to be quite Healthy and Happy without any Drugs, Tractors nor Cars. {See: **"The Great False Economy is now DEBUNKED!" (Adolf Hitler had a much Better Economic System!), Book 053, plus: "The United States of the Whole World!" (A True Global Economy for the Masses of Working People!), Book 055, plus: "The New RIGHTEOUS One-World Government!" (HOW to Establish a Righteous One-World Government without Going to WAR!) By The Worldwide People's Revolution!® Book 056.**}

04-09 [_] Well, if I Recall Correctly, it seems that Jesus had something to say about that. Yes, it was to the Effect that if something so Precious to you as your own Right Eye, is Offending you, it is Best for you to Pluck it Out and Throw it Away from you. (See *Matthew 5:29.*) However, no one's Eyes ever Offended the Possessor of them: beCause they are Precious Things that everyone Needs for Seeing what is on the Ingredient Labels of those Packages for Sale in the Gross Grocery Stores, which are Loaded with Abominations, which are not Fit for Hogs to Eat. Therefore, if that Television is Offending you, why do you not Change the Channel, or Watch some Educational DVD's, or something that is Uplifting and Edifying, rather than Watch something that is Depressing and Negative — such as those Ball Games, where there are always Losers? Why not Read some Good Books, which might Inspire you to Say and Do GOOD Things?

04-10 [_] Trust me, O Selected King, I have Tried Reading the *Bible* with a Capital R, only to be more and more Depressed by it: beCause of the Outlandish LIES in it, which makes it no more Trustworthy than the Wicked Federal Government of **"The Divided States of United Lies,"** which seems to have Gathered up the Worst of its Ideas from the *Bible,* itself, whereby those Republicans Imagine themselves to be Ancient Israelites, who are supposed to Conquer the World — at least Financially and Economically. However, it seems that the World is Conquering us! Yes, we are the Losers in almost every Transaction, and our Jobs have gone Overseas: beCause of Cheap Labor over there, whereby American Businessmen can now get Richer by Moving OUT of **"The Divided States of United Lies!"** Halleluiah! Praise Buzzeldick the Great! And I am not Totally Insane, yet; but, I am Working on it. †§‡§§

— Chapter 05 —

Working Soldiers do not have to Tell Lies!

05-01 [_] So, what if a Working Soldier is a Natural Born Liar: beCause of being the Son of a Capitalist Hog, who Habitually Earned his Living by Deceptions and Lies, being a Kind of Half-breed Snake, crossed with a Sunday Church-going Sheep, or Wolf in Sheep's Clothing, as Jesus put it, who Sings Praises to some Imaginary God, who Loved the People of the Whole World so much that he Gave to us Hordes of Mosquitoes with Malaria, which Kills upwards of a Million Innocent Children per Year — HOW are you going to keep him from Lying? †§‡

05-02 [_] Well, it is True that a lot of People would have to be Converted to the Truth, whatever it might be, so as to not be Lying Hypocrites; but, that is another Subject.

05-03 [_] Suppose some Working Soldier gets Lazy, and puts only one Bucket of Cement in the Concrete Mixer, when he is supposed to put 2 five-gallon Buckets in it for each Batch of Concrete — HOW will such a Liar be Detected and Punished for it?

05-04 [_] Well, if he is Mixing up Concrete for his own House, it is Doubtful that he will Want to Cheat on the Cement: beCause that would greatly Weaken the Concrete, and thus Ruin his own House. However, if he is a Normal Capitalist, who is Mixing Concrete for someone else's House, it is very Tempting to Cheat on the Cement: beCause it is Expensive Stuff, whereby the Cheater might Gain several thousands of Dollars on just one Project. After all, one can hardly tell by the Appearance of Concrete whether or not it has the Right Amount of Cement. Moreover, one can hardly tell just how much Concrete is in a Concrete Truck, when the "Ready-mixed" Concrete is Delivered by the Capitalist Cheater: beCause you cannot See all of it within the Truck, which can be Dumped into a Concrete Pump, whereby the Cheaters can Gain thousands of Dollars. For Example, I was Charged for several Loads of Concrete that were never Delivered: beCause the Capitalist Cheaters got another Concrete Job lined up at the same Time, which was half-way between my Property and the Company that did the Delivering of the Concrete, whereby the Truckers simply stopped by that other Place, and Dumped Out half or more of the Concrete before they Drove on to my Worksite, where they Dumped the Remaining Concrete into the Pump on the Truck, where it Disappeared into the Hole, whereby there was no Way to Measure it. Therefore, it Required about 14 Truckloads of Concrete, instead of the Pre-calculated 7 Loads! Therefore, without Realizing what was Happening: beCause of being Inexperienced, I got Robbed by Capitalist Criminals, whom I Trusted! ‡

05-05 [_] So, O Selected King, could you not have taken the Case to Court, and Won a BIG Lawsuit, which would have Paid for the Concrete Work, several Times over, whereby you might have even Retired on it, in Hawaii? †§‡

05-06 [_] Well, I made the Mistake of Trusting the Concrete Workers, instead of Watching them like a Hawk. Indeed, I had no Idea that they might have been Pulling Tricks on me. After all, this is America — "the Greatest Nation on the Earth," as Mr. Congressman said, and I was Naïve enough to Believe that Lie, which would never have Happened in Germany: beCause they are Honest Hardworking People, who would never Cheat on anything, which is WHY they almost Won the Second World War, while Americans would have most Certainly Lost that War, if Adolf Hitler had simply put his Armies to WORK, Building those **GLORIOUS Swanky Hotels Castles and Fortresses,** whereby all of the Germans could have gotten Moderately RICH, without Losing the Life of even ONE Working Soldier! Indeed, the Idea must not have crossed his Mind: beCause of being Blinded by PRIDE. (See *Proverbs 16:18.*) Nevertheless, it is Doubtful that I could have Won a Lawsuit: beCause there was no Way to Prove just how Large the Volume of Space was in the Hole that got Filled with Concrete, without Digging it all up; and I had no Desire to do that: beCause it would have Ruined the whole Project.

05-07 [_] So, O Selected King, if Adolf Hitler had been a Wise Man, like King Solomon, he would have simply put his Armies to WORK, Building those Beautiful Planned City States, whereby it would have been Impossible for the Russians, French, British, Americans, or anyone else to make War Against him, huh? Why did he not have Faith in the National Socialist German Workers' Party (NSDAP), and just Forget about going to War?

05-08 [_] Well, if you Study my Plans for those Beautiful Planned City States, you will Realize just how Impractical it would be to Attempt to Conquer any such City, even with Hydrogen Bombs: beCause of the Mountainous Buildings, which would be Spread Out over Miles of Territory; and every House would be like a Miniature Fortress within itself, which would be more Difficult to Conquer than Heinrich Himmler's House in Berlin, whereby 6 Men Defended it against the Russians, who Lost some 240+ Men, just to Defeat those 6 Brave Warriors at a Time when German Children were also Fighting: beCause they were so Greatly Outnumbered by the Russians, who had 22 Million Soldiers Fighting only 750,000 Germans, and nearly Lost the Battle! †‡

05-09 [_] It does seem like the Germans are by far the Better Strategists, huh?

05-10 [_] Well, if they are, they should now take up the Construction of those Beautiful Planned City States: beCause those Cities have no less than 5,000 Good Reasons and Great Advantages for Building them and Living within the Borders of them, with NO Great Disadvantages! {See www.Amazon.com for: **"The Right Design for Living!" (A List of Great Advantages for Building Beautiful Planned City States!)**, Book 012, plus: **"GLORIOUS Swanky Hotels**

Castles and Fortresses!" (Beautiful Planned City States for WISE Intelligent Well-Educated People with Common Sense and Good Understanding!) By The Worldwide People's Revolution!® Book 019.}

— Chapter 06 —

Good Soldiers are Working Soldiers!

06-01 [_] So, WHO would do all of the Slave Labor for the Construction of all such HUGE Swanky Fortresses, which might be 100 Miles or more in Diameter and a Mile High?

06-02 [_] Well, most of the "Slave Labor" would be done by Bulldozers, Earth Moving Machines, Rock Quarrying Machines, Rock Cutting Machines, Rock Polishing Machines, Front-end Loaders, Cranes, Trains, Huge Concrete Mixers, Solar-powered Cement Factories, Water Ships, and other Heavy Equipment, whereby there would be a Minimum Amount of Difficult Work for anyone to do. Indeed, those "Mechanical Beasts" will never Complain about Low Wages, will never go on Strike, and will Cost far less than War Machines — such as those 250 Billion-dollar Jet Bombers, and Trillion-dollar Aircraft Carriers, Submarines, War Ships, Army Tanks, and all such Horribly Expensive Equipment, whereby Satan and Sons, Incorporated, have made themselves very Rich. Yes, their Day of Glory is about to come to an END! †§‡

06-03 [_] So, O Selected King, do you Actually Believe that most People will LEAVE their Cities of Confusion, and Move into Beautiful Planned City States: beCause of Reason and Logic? Indeed, I have noticed that it is Difficult to Persuade even Poor Homeless People to leave their Flea-infested Lice Dens in the Subways and Sewage Systems of New Yuck City: beCause of getting Used to it, and even Bonded to it. Therefore, HOW are you going to Persuade them to Join one of **Seven Great Swanky Armies of Voluntary Working Soldiers**? †§‡

06-04 [_] Well, if all such People are Offered GOOD Swanky Wages — such as 60$ per Hour for Setting Marble Tiles on the Walls of their own Beautiful Stone Dome Homes, they are likely to Spring Back to Life, and Rise Up Early during the Cool Time of the Morning, and do their 4 Hours of Common Skilled Labor, just to get that 60 Dollars per Hour, most of which would be Kept in Reserve for them: so that they can Buy their own Beautiful Stone Dome Home Complexes with only 6 Years of Common Unskilled Labor, whereby they will Obtain large Comfortable Living Rooms, which are 24 to 30 feet in diameter, which are Attached to Kitchen Domes that are 16 to 20 feet in diameter, which are Attached to Walk-in Cooler and Freezer Domes, which are 20 to 24 feet in diameter, which are Attached by Barrel-vault Tunnels to their Luscious All-Mineral Organic Gardens, each of which is no less than 210 feet by 210 feet: so that each Family can have its own Fruit Trees, Nut Trees, Vegetable Gardens, Vineyard, and Flower Gardens: so as to be Able to Feed themselves and others, without Depending on Government Welfare Programs, nor the Salvation Army. Indeed, they will be Provided with all of the Necessary Tools, Compost, Rock Minerals, Mulching Rocks, and everything Needed for GOOD Gardening, without any Loans, without any Interest, and without any Taxes: beCause none of those Evil Things are Needed for True Prosperity. †‡ {See: **"A List of FAIR Swanky Wages!"** (The Equitable Wage System!), Book 065, plus: **"The LUSCIOUS All-Mineral Organic Method of Gardening!"** (HOW to **Grow DELICIOUS Satisfying Foods for Potential Kingz and Kweenz in Swanky PALACES!) By The Worldwide People's Revolution!®**, Book 021, which is a Companion Book of: **"Orgimmick Gardening at its Best!"** (HOW to Grow Delicious Satisfying Foods **without a 10-Million-Dollar Investment!) By The Worldwide People's Revolution!® B-079.**}

06-05 [_] I Object, your Honor: beCause we would have to Collect Taxes, just to Build all such Beautiful Planned City States! †§‡

06-06 [_] NOT if you Elect me to be your Righteous King: beCause I will simply Command the New RIGHTEOUS One-World GovernMINT to Mint and Print the Necessary New Money for HIRING all of the Working Soldiers to Build all such Beautiful Planned City States; and therefore, those Stone Walls will Represent that New Money, which will make it the very Best Money in all of the World: beCause it will have to be Earned by Honest Labor, without any Loans, without any Interest / Usury, and without any Taxes! ‡ {See: **"The CONSTITUTION for the New RIGHTEOUS One-World GovernMINT!"** (HOW all Peoples can get True Justice, and **Celebrate the Great Year of JUBILEE!) By The Worldwide People's Revolution!® B-016.**}

06-07 [_] So, if there are no Taxes, WHO will Pay the Policemen to Guard us, until all such Cities are Finished? Moreover, WHO will Pay the Teachers to Teach to us HOW to Do the Building, since we know nothing yet as we ought to Know for True Prosperity?

06-08 [_] Well, before I will Hire anyone to Build anything, we must SEPARATE the Good Honest Hardworking People from the Thieves, Liars, Robbers, and other Criminals, which we can do by each Person Filling Out and Filing **"The Complete SURVEYS of our VALUES!"** (SURVEYS **of Religious Spiritual Political Governmental Sexual Social Moral Economic Business Labor Habitual and Miscellaneous VALUES!) By The Worldwide People's Revolution!®**, Book 059. After all, there is no Need for Taxing Hardworking Honest People to Support Criminals, when it is Possible for the Criminals to Support themselves and others — such as Orphans, Old Widows, Mentally Deranged People, and Helpless People, which will Require a Voluntary TITHE of 10% of their Incomes, which they may also Use to Hire Policemen, if it does not cross their Minds that there is no Need for Policemen, at all, IF everyone simply Learns, Believes, Loves, and OBEYS **"The New MAGNIFIED Version of the 20 Commandments,"** which can be found in **"LIGHTNING STRIKES Versus Lightning Bugs!"** (HOW you can Become Moderately **RICH, without Telling any Lies nor Selling any Trash) By The Worldwide People's Revolution!®**, Book 074, on www.Amazon.com, along with: **"WHO QUALIFIES to Rule Over US?"** Yes, you will Discover the Truth, and that Truth will make you FREE with a Capital F when you Practice it! ‡

06-09 [_] It seems as if I have Heard this same Song, before, O Selected King; but, suppose we do not WANT to Leave our Glorious Cities of Confusion: beCause of Loving those Rapists, Robbers, Thieves, Liars, Murderers, Prostitutes, Drug Dealers, Tax Collectors, Brutal Policemen, Government Snoops, and whatever might be Found in all such Glorious Cities? †§‡§§

06-10 [_] Well, in that Case, you may Continue to Live wherever you Love it. However, when all of the Righteous People Pack Up their Rags and Bags and MOVE AWAY, Things will have a Tendency to get much Worse than they are, whereby you will come to your Right Senses with the Prodigal Son of *Luke 15*. Guaranteed! {See: **"The New MAGNIFIED Version of the GOOD NEWS According to Saint LUKE!" (The Magnified Gospel of Luke in Plain English!) By The Worldwide People's Revolution!®** Book 061.}

— Chapter 07 —

Good Soldiers are Cooperative

07-01 [_] So, O Selected King of **The Worldwide People's Revolution!®**, what makes you Vainly Imagine that any Government in this World of Confusion will ALLOW you to Form a Righteous State within any other State? Are you not Aware that such an Act is Unconstitutional?

07-02 [_] Well, I have read **"The CONSTITUTION for the New RIGHTEOUS One-World GovernMINT,"** several Times, and have yet to Discover any such Silly law. After all, it is Understandable WHY such a law was written within the Constitution for **the Divided States of United Lies**: beCause they did not Want any Group of People to be Free from Taxes, whereby they might Live like Kings and Queens in **"Beautiful Swanky PALACES"**: beCause of Loving and Obeying the above Mentioned Constitution, which Explains **HOW all Peoples can get True Justice, and Celebrate the Great Year of JUBILEE!** Yes, that might Sound Impossible to someone who has not Studied that Inspiring Book; but, for those who are Wise People, who have Studied it, it seems to be most Reasonable and Logical. It is Book 016, which is a Companion Book of: **"The Great World TEMPLE of PEACE!" (The Glory of Jerusalem Arises Again!) By The Worldwide People's Revolution!®** Book 017.

07-03 [_] So, O Selected King, it seems that you are quite Confident that X-amount of Potential Working Soldiers will just DROP their Present Jobs, and take up their Picks and Shovels, and begin to DIG IN, huh? Did you not say in some other uninspired book that those Stone Dome Homes would be Covered with 10 to 20 feet of DIRT, which will all have to be Shoveled, by HAND into the Bucket of a Crane, which moves 12 Tons at a Time? †§‡§§

07-04 [_] You must have Skipped Over a Previous Chapter, which clearly Explained HOW MACHINES WILL DO MOST OF THE SLAVE LABOR — that is, IF I am Elected to be your Righteous KING, who will just Command it to be Done, with or without the Approval of any Congressional IDIOTS, who are Working for the Synagogue of Satan, who have made Education Slaves, Work Slaves, Tax Slaves, Interest Slaves, Insurance Slaves, Drug Slaves, and Endless Bills Slaves of almost all of you Silly IGNORANT People, who have been Greatly Deceived by the Election Deceptions, whereby you have been Voting for one of 2 or 3 WRong Political Parties for Centuries, and you are still Poor Wretched Miserable SLAVES, who do not even have Fresh Clean Air to Breathe, Pure Living Water to Drink, Wholesome Natural Foods to Eat, Proper Natural

Clothing to Wear, Secure Insurance-proof Self-air-conditioned Houses to Live in, nor even Gardens to Feed yourselves, much less Spacious Home-craft Workshops with the Best of German-made Tools and Sales Shops, which would be Joining your Stone Dome Home Complexes by Means of Barrel-vault Tunnels, Elevators, Escalators, Subway Electric Trains, and whatever is Needed for True Prosperity, and without Borrowing any Money from anyone. ‡

07-05 [_] So, O Selected King, WHO would OWN all such Beautiful Planned City States, until we Collected enough Money for Buying them, at Cost?

07-06 [_] Well, the New RIGHTEOUS One-World GovernMINT would Naturally Own all such Cities, until People Pay for them, at Cost, which will only be the Cost of LABOR: beCause all of the Building Materials will be Cheerfully DONATED by WE, the People, who will Claim our own Mountains of Rocks, Rivers of Water, Sand, Gravel, and whatever we Need, who will Learn HOW to Cooperate with one another, as one large Happy Family, or else the Master Farmer is going to STOP the Rain on all of the Land, and CURSE US! Therefore, we have 3 Options:

    A-[_] Cooperate as Loving Brothers and Sisters should, and thus Build Swanky Fortresses;

    B-[_] Reject the Provable Truths, and be Blasted Away with Hydrogen and Atomic Bombs, or:

    C-[_] Commit Suicide.

07-07 [_] I much Prefer that everything just Continues as it is, even if we do not have Fresh Clean Air to Breathe, Pure Living Water to Drink, Wholesome Natural Foods to Eat, Natural Clothing to Wear, Secure Fire-proof Termite-proof Hail-proof Rot-proof Paint-proof Tornado-proof Insurance-proof Tax-proof nor Self-air-conditioned Houses to Live in: beCause I LOVE all of my BILLS, and can hardly wait to get some more Bills to Pay, which make me SO HAPPY! HalulqYU! Praaz Buzouldik thu Graat! †§‡§§

07-08 [_] You must be a Real Dimwitcrat, or a Reprobate from Hell. Therefore, may you get the Desires of your Heart, and Suffer with the Seven Last Great Plagues! †§‡

07-09 [_] I am going to Heaven when I Die; and therefore, it does not Worry me.

07-10 [_] Be Advised with the Warnings of the Most High God, himself, who has Assured us that this Earth is our Eternal Home, unless we are Cast Down to a Lower Order of Worlds, which are Seven Times more Evil than here! {See www.Amazon.com for: **"God Speaks and the Whole World Listens!" (Fire on the Mountain from the Burning Bush by the Spirit of Truth!)**, Book 026, plus: **"HOW to Get our PRIORITIES in ORDER!" (The Glories of Democracy; and, Does DEMON-ocracy have its Priorities in Order?) By The Worldwide People's Revolution!® Book 060.**}

— Chapter 08 —

Good Soldiers will Educate themselves!

08-01 [_] O Selected King of **The Worldwide People's Revolution!®**, I must Confess that I have never "red" more Interesting Books than your Inspired Books; but, I am Greatly Worried for those Jobless Graduates of the Schools of Ignorant Fools, who are "Burned Out" on Reading, you might say, who have no more *Interest* in reading any books, much less any Inspired Books, such as: **"Are you a Jobless Graduate of the SKQL uv FQLZ?" (How to get a GOUD EJUKAASHUN without Robbing the Bank!) By The Worldwide People's Revolution!®** Book 020. Therefore, what is to be Done for them, since they are Suicidal? After all, when you come Out of College with a Master's Degree in Mental Rapeology, being no less than 100,000$ in DEBT, without even a Boring Job in some Eatery, Flipping Hamburgers, for Example, what are you supposed to DO — get into the Book Selling Business? †§‡

08-02 [_] Well, if you have Suffered in your State of Extreme Poverty, long enough, it might not be a Bad Idea to Sell my Inspired Books: beCause, not everyone is Spiritually DEAD! In Fact, some People are doing quite Well with the Sales of my Inspired Books: beCause they Especially Appeal to POOR Deprived People, who only have to Sacrifice a Meal or 2, whereby they can Afford to Buy such a Book as this one, which will Satisfy their Souls much more than any Meal of Hog Slop or Dog Food at the Death and Hell Rest and Rot Shop. Therefore, if you are Extremely Poor, you can begin by Selling just this one Book on Street Corners where Poor People are passing by, just by Announcing the Full Title of the Book, LOUD and Clear, including the Pen Name of your Selected King, just to get their Attention, which is **The Worldwide People's Revolution!®** Yes, "Poor Nigger Jim" and "Huck Finn" will LOVE IT. After all, they have no Desire to become Potential Murderers in some Hateful War, just to Earn their Livings. Therefore, for Example, you could Stand Up and Hold Up a Copy of this Book in your Right Hand, and Shout Out with Great Boldness, LOUD and Clear: **"Does a Good Soldier have to be a MURDERER?" (Seven Great Swanky Armies of Voluntary Working Soldiers!) By The Worldwide People's Revolution!®** {See www.Amazon.com for: **"The Washington Journal is a FARCE!" (C-SPAN Managers are not very WISE!) By The Worldwide People's Revolution!®** Book 006. You may use the Name of any Selected King that you Like, if someone Wants to Learn WHO your Selected King is, who may also Sign the Book with his Name, if you can Persuade him to do so. After all, who in his or her Riit Miind can Deny the Truths within it? John McArdle of the *Washington Journal* Fame certainly would not. See the C-SPAN TV Network on the Internet.}

08-03 [_] O Selected King, I find that Poor People are more Interested in: **"LIGHTNING Versus the Lightning Bug!" (HOW almost Everyone can become Moderately RICH, without Telling Any Lies nor Selling Any Trash!) By The Worldwide People's Revolution!®**, Book 001: beCause there are no Colored Photographs within that Book, while **"LIGHTNING STRIKES Versus Lightning Bugs"** has more than 60 Photos, which makes that Book Cost a lot more; but, the Information is somewhat the same. Yes, they are a bit Puzzled by the Main Title; but, none of them have any Trouble Understanding the Subtitle — except that many of them do not Believe it, until they read the first 30 Pages or so; and then they are Fully Persuaded that you do Speak the TRUTH.

08-04 [_] O Selected King, I much Prefer to Sell: **"GOOD NEWS for REBEL WOMEN!" (How almost all Wives can become Moderately RICH without Leaving their Homes! Guaranteed!)** Book 010. However, the Book that all People should Read with a Capital R is called: **"Poverty Hunger Riots Strikes Brutalities Election Deceptions and Civil Wars!" (The High Price that we Earthlings have Paid for Leaving the Good Land!) By The Worldwide People's Revolution!®** Book 014.

08-05 [_] Well, all of my Inspired Books are very Good, and some of them are more Appealing to certain Classes of People — both Rich and Poor — Depending on just how much Schooling that they have had, whereby they might Understand all of the Words, and thus Appreciate them. However, when it comes to my "Funetik Ingglish," most People have to be Assisted by a Teacher for an Hour or so, just to get the "Hang" of it. Nevertheless, you can Challenge the most Educated People with it, just to Discover that they are not nearly as Smart as some 8-year-old Children, who have more Faith in it, who can often read it right off without any Lessons at all. {See www.Amazon.com for: **"The Public School of IGNERUNT FQLZ!" (How we have been GRAATLEE DISEEVD by Capitalism!)**, Book 024, which Teaches HOW to "Reed" it, plus: **"In thu Beeginingz uv Thingz!" (Thu Kreeaashun Stooree frum thu Beegining!) By The Worldwide People's Revolution!®**, Book 025, which is mostly written in "Funetik Ingglish," which is one of the most Enlightening Books in the World. Otherwise, you might want to check out: **"Thu Nq MAGNUFIID Verzhun uv Thu PROVERBZ uv KING SOLUMUN in Plaan Ingglish!" (The Understandable Version of the Famous Proverbs of King Solomon in Plain English!) By The Worldwide People's Revolution!®** Book 028.

08-06 [_] I much Prefer to Sell: **"God Speaks and the Whole World Listens!" (Fire on the Mountain from the Burning Bush by the Spirit of Truth!)**, Book 026; or, **"The UGLY Scarred Dishonest Face of Poor Old Miserable UNCLE SAM!" (A Memorial Day Legacy!) By The Worldwide People's Revolution!®**, Book 054, which contains 2 Special Epistles to Saint John McArdle of the *Washington Journal*. {See YouTube Videos for: "THE NEW WORLD ORDER — A 6000 Year History — HD FEATURE.}

08-07 [_] Well, whichever Books you like to Sell, you can be Sure that there will be many other People who will Like them, and will also be seen on the Streets, now and then, with their own Copies to Sell: beCause of my Generous Offer to KEEP 90% of the Net Profits for themselves, according to my Instructions in: **"LIGHTNING Versus the Lightning Bug!"** Book 001. †§‡

08-08 [_] So, O Selected King, is it Fair to say that 4 Competing Salesmen could Sell more Books on any given Street Corner, than just one Salesman?

08-09 [_] Well, I would say that 4 People on 4 Joining Corners could Sell more Books than 4 People who are Scattered Out throughout any given City: beCause of getting the Attention of the Potential Buyers. In Fact, if just one really Good-looking Person had a High Price on a given Book, and another less-Beautiful Salesman had a Lower Price on the same Book, more Books would Sell. Another Plan is to Sell several Books at their Normal Prices, while having a "Special Sale" on just one Book, such as this one, whereby the Customers might be Enticed to Buy more of them from you, if the Prices are just a bit Lower than they are in www.Amazon.com, right now. †‡

08-10 [_] So, it is Obvious that People must get Interested in the Great Truths that are Taught in your Inspired Books, before they will get Interested in Buying them, huh?

— Chapter 09 —

Good Soldiers are not Afraid to Learn New Lessons!

09-01 [_] O Selected King of **The Worldwide People's Revolution!®**, there is a Great Question that someone Asked in Verse 00-10 — What if we do not Believe the New MAGNIFIED Version of the *Scriptures*? What if we Live by the King James Authorized Version, only, and Disregard all other Versions — will we still be Judged According to whatever Provable Truths might be Found in the New MAGNIFIED Version? Will you please Answer that Question for us?

09-02 [_] Well, we can only be Judged by whatever we have Learned. Therefore, if you have never "red" the New MAGNIFIED Version (NMV), you could hardly be held Accountable for whatever might be in it. However, a Good Soldier is not a Spiritual Coward. Therefore, he is not Afraid to Learn New Lessons, even if he must Trash all of his Old Beliefs and Vain Traditions, if they have been Proven to be WRong. ‡

09-03 [_] What if we are Convicted that Driving Gas-hog Cars is WRong — will we go to Hell for Continuing to Drive such Cars?

09-04 [_] Well, God will not Condemn you for Driving such Cars, if you just Confess that it is WRong to do so, and Help to Enlighten the Minds of your Friends, Relatives, and Naaberz, with whom you can Share this Inspired Book, which will Remind them that, *"To him who Knows to Do Good, and he does not Do it, to him it is a Sin." — James 4:17.* Therefore, once you Know *that* for a Fact, which you now Know, there is no Escaping from the Judgment Day. Indeed, you Instinctively Know that it is WRong to Pollute the Air, Water, and Land with any Kind of an Abomination — such as Gasoline and Motor Oils, which contain Lead, Mercury, Arsenic, Cadmium, and other Toxic Poisons, which are best left in the Ground, where they Belong: beCause there are Non-toxic much-less-Expensive Means of Transportation — such as Walking, Riding a Horse, Bicycle, Tricycle, Quadruped, Elevator, or Electric Train, which can be Powered by the Sunlight, Wind, and Running Water, whereby Pollution can be Reduced to a Minimum Amount, and not Lower your Standard of Living by even one Degree: beCause of getting up and going to Work at HOME, or near Home, in your own LUSCIOUS All-Mineral Organic Garden, Vineyard, Orchard, or Home-craft Workshop and Sales Shop, which I will be Happy to Help you to Build. {See www.Amazon.com for: **"The LUSCIOUS All-Mineral Organic Method of Gardening!" (HOW to Grow DELICIOUS Satisfying Foods for Potential Kingz and Kweenz in Swanky PALACES!) By The Worldwide People's Revolution!®** Books 021 and 079.

09-05 [_] O Selected King, if only a certain Percentage of us Americans DID what you have Proposed, the Great False Economy would CRASH! And then we would all be OUT of Work! †‡

09-06 [_] How in the World could anyone be Out of Work, when we have Millions of Beautiful Planned City States to be BUILT? Can you not HEAR anything, O Deaf Cow?

09-07 [_] Can you not Hear anything, O Unelected King? Almost no one is going to go along with your Master Plan, even if it is a Utopian Idea, whose Time has now Come: beCause, "a Bird in the Hand is Worth 3 in the Bushes." In other words, People are not Willing to Gamble on your Master Plan, when they already have a Capitalist Thread to Hang onto, even if you Offer to them a very Strong *Rope of Hope* that no one can Break by any Means, even if the People of the entire World were Clinging to it! Indeed, they are Afraid to let go of that Rotten Capitalist Thread, which is about to Break, anyway. †§‡

09-08 [_] Well, that is WHY it is very Important to SPREAD the Truths that I Teach as Quickly as Possible: so that the Great False Economy does not have Time to Crash, before **"The New RIGHTEOUS One-World Government"** is Established, which will make a Smooth Transition from one Lifestyle to another. After all, if my Master Plan is Followed, everyone will just Continue to Work at whatever Jobs that they are now Working at; but, all of the Unemployed People and Underemployed People will Immediately go to Work at those **GLORIOUS Swanky Hotels Castles and Fortresses!** Yes, they might even have to Live in TENTS for awhile, until some Hotels can be Built for them. However, as more and more Rooms are Finished, more and more People will be Able to Move in, who can Share their Rooms, until they get more Houses Finished in the Fortresses, which will be a New Experience for many People; but, it will only be Temporary. Moreover, those People will be called "PIONEERS": beCause of "Paving the Way" for others to Follow. Therefore, if you Want to Join **"The Swanky Association of PIONEERS,"** and go to Work, Immediately, you can now begin to Sell my Inspired Books by whatever Means might Work. Just be Sure to be Honest, Friendly, Kind, Respectful, Patient, and Trustworthy.

09-09 [_] I would like to Sell your Inspired Books, O Selected King; but, I am Afraid that I might be Persecuted for it: beCause you are not Exactly Popular among Rich People, who might even have me Assassinated by some Thugs.

09-10 [_] Well, in your Case, I would say that you need to Team Up with some Friends, who can Stick Together and Protect each other: beCause there is Strength in Numbers, which Means that you need to be Uniformed Working Soldiers, who Appear to be American Soldiers, Sailors, Airmen, Marines, or whatever; but, with Cowboy Hats on, or Black Mennonite Hats, all of the same Color and Kind: so as to Maintain your Uniformity, which will Help to Draw some Attention to yourselves, which will Open Up a Door for more Conversations with your Potential Customers, whom you can Encourage to "Reed" this Inspired Book, or whatever Books that you are Attempting to Sell. After all, they make a Wonderful Display when all of the Books are all Lined Up, 10 in a Row, in 4 Rows on a Sheet of ¾-inch Plywood, which rests on a 2-feet-high Stand. You can find Better Instructions in: **"God Speaks and the Whole World Listens!" (Fire on the Mountain from the Burning Bush by the Spirit of Truth!)**, Book 026; and in: **"GOOD NEWS for REBEL WOMEN!" (HOW almost all Wives can become Moderately RICH without Leaving their Homes! Guaranteed!) By The Worldwide People's Revolution!® Book 010.** Be Sure to Build Up your Muscles with some Exercises: so at to Appear to be Real Working Soldiers, even if you are not yet Building Swanky Fortresses, which will also Help you to get Prepared for it. After all, nothing is more Appealing to People than Well-built Bodies, which will also give to you a Natural Sense of Security. Therefore, do some Push Ups and Pull Ups, and thus get yourself Looking Good. Also, Invite some other Body Builders to Help you to Sell the Books. SMILE, be Friendly, and Perfectly Honest. For Example, if someone Asks you how you got your Big Muscles, you should tell them Exactly how. Do not Say nor Do anything that you might be Ashamed of later on, if the Truth should be Discovered by someone.

— Chapter 10 —

Good Soldiers are Teachable!

10-01 [_] O Selected King of **The Worldwide People's Revolution!®**, I Dread the Thoughts of having to Learn New Lessons — such as **"The LUSCIOUS All-Mineral Organic Method of Gardening!" (HOW to Grow DELICIOUS Satisfying Foods for Potential Kingz and Kweenz in Swanky PALACES!)** Book 021. In Fact, I am TERRIFIED by the Thoughts of it. §

10-02 [_] Well, there is actually nothing to be Afraid of: beCause there will be Good Teachers to Help you to Learn all such Lessons, even if it Requires Months of Training. After all, **"The Swanky Associations of Working Soldiers"** are not going to allow you to Starve to Death, if they have anything to Eat, and the entire **Second Army of Working Soldiers** will be Dedicated to Growing and Preserving Foods. {See www.Amazon.com for: **"Seven Great Armies of Working Soldiers!" (HOW to Provide a Way for Everyone to WORK: so as to Eliminate Poverty, Crimes, Drug Abuses, Prisons and Unnecessary Taxes!)**, Book 015, plus: **"The Swanky Associations of Working Soldiers!" (A Fascinating Collection of Various Kinds of Voluntary Working Soldiers!) By The Worldwide People's Revolution!®** Book 018.}

10-03 [_] So, O Selected King, WHY is the Subtitle of this Inspired Book not Different, since it is the same as the Title of your other Book?

10-04 [_] Well, if you Study the Words Carefully, you will notice that there is a slight Difference, and that Difference is actually a very BIG Difference: beCause "Swanky" makes them Special, as in "First Class Quality." Indeed, the First Army of Voluntary Working Soldiers will be Book Sellers, since that is what is most Needed at this Time, in Order to Spread the Seeds of Truths as Quickly as Possible, and Relentlessly so: beCause the Masses of People, Worldwide, must Learn about my Master Plan at about the same Time, in Order to make it most Effective: beCause of making it a Great Controversy, such as the World has never Witnessed before now. In Fact, I call it a "Forest Fire of Truths," which must be "Kindled" all around the World, in any "Dry Forests" that are "Burnable," wherever there is any Unemployment, Discontentment, Unrest, Riots, Strikes, Hunger, Poverty, or whatever. Yes, all such "Trees" must be "Lit on Fire" by the "Burning Bush," itself, which is most Powerful in this Case: beCause it is an almost Unquenchable FIRE, which cannot easily be Extinguished, once it is Burning, even in a "Wet Forest," which has been

"Soaked" with Propagandist Lies, as in the "American Dream" Case, which was a very Bad Dream from the Beginning: beCause American Houses are Designed for Destruction, which anyone would Naturally Realize, if they only Studied the Latest News Reports about House Fires, Tornado Destructions, Hurricane Disasters, Floods, Mudslides, and whatever. Otherwise, they could go on the Internet, and Search in Google for "Images | Hurricanes | Tornadoes" for whatever might be in there to Persuade them. Indeed, it is rather Frightening to Live in such a House, which can be Silently Buried under an Ice Storm during just one Dreadful Night, which can have Ice a foot deep on the Roof by the Morning, whereby all such Dangerous Houses can simply Collapse! Moreover, if that Ice were 2 Feet Deep, you could rest assured that no Traffic would be Moving during the Morning: beCause most of the People would be DEAD, or DYING: beCause of their Roofs Caving IN, even on their Cars. Therefore, without any ElecTrickery, they could not Survive for very long — Thanks to those Bankers, who would not Loan any Money for Building Proper Houses: beCause they Work Hand-in-Hand with those Insurance Agencies, who Belong to the same Clan of Lying Zionist Edomites, who Belong to the Synagogue of Satan, who Pledge their Allegiance to a Bloody Rag, and Disregard the Divine Laws of the Master Farmer, who will have the Last Laugh when their Unholy Kingdom comes to a Sudden END! {See: **"The END of CONFUSION!" (The Great CELEBRATION of the Magnificent Wedding of the Most Humble Honest Nations, and the Grand Year of JUBILEE!) By The Worldwide People's Revolution!®** Book 050.}

10-05 [_] So, O Selected King, it appears that you have Proven that the Normal American is a Foolish GAMBLER, who Gambles with his or her Life, every Night, while Sleeping: beCause it is Possible for all such Houses to Collapse during Ice Storms, or Burn Up with Fires, Wash Away with Floods, get Blown Away by Tornadoes, Buried Under Mudslides and Volcanoes, or Sunk into Holes that are made by Earthquakes. However, just Exactly what are the Chances of any such Things Actually Happening to ME?

10-06 [_] Well, all such Things have been Happening to Americans for hundreds of Years, whereby hundreds of thousands of them have Died, or Lost practically everything they Owned; and yet few Americans have Learned any Lessons from such Things, whereby they might have Changed their Minds, and Concluded that only Swanky FORTRESSES are Safe Places to Live in. {See: **"The IDEAL Place to Live!" (HOW to Discover the Ideal Place to Live!),** Book 069, plus: **"Has your Life become Extremely Complicated?" (HOW to Live a SIMPLE Life!) By The Worldwide People's Revolution!®** Book 068.}

10-07 [_] You have to have something in your "Coconut" besides Water, before you can Learn.

10-08 [_] Well, sometimes People have to Suffer SEVERE Disasters before they can be Taught anything. Indeed, some of them must Suffer SEVERE Sicknesses, or Diseases, before they come to their Right Senses with the Prodigal Son of *Luke 15*. {See www.Amazon.com for: **"Did God or Satan Ordain Medical Doctors??" (Ask Huck Finn and/or Nigger Jim: because neither Tom Sawyer nor Judge Thatcher would Know!) By The Worldwide People's Revolution!®** Book 022.}

10-09 [_] I much Prefer to Learn my Lessons the most Easiest Way Possible, which is to Learn them from Wise Men of Ancient Times.

10-10 [_] Well, you are Wise to do that; but, if you Study my Inspired Books, Carefully, you will Discover that I have Far more Wisdom than they had; and I am not saying that to Brag about it; but, just to state the Facts. {See the above Link for: **"Thu Nq MAGNUFIED Verzhun uv Thu PROVERBZ uv KING SOLUMUN in Plaan Ingglish!"** (**The Understandable Version of the Famous Proverbs of King Solomon in Plain English!**), Book 028, plus: **"ECCLESIASTES UNCOVERED!"** (**The New MAGNIFIED Version of Ecclesiastes and the Song of Solomon in Plain English!**) **By The Worldwide People's Revolution!® Book 034.**}

— Chapter 11 —

Working Soldiers can Sleep in Peace!

11-01 [_] I have Actually been in a War, in Vietnam; and therefore, I know what it is like to have myself Woke Up during the Night by Mortars EXPLODING, or by Weapons Firing Bullets, whereby I am still Shaken by such Noises, even 48+ Years later! Therefore, I Testify that all such Evil Things are no Good for a Person's Nerves, much less for a Person's Good Health. However, that Unjust War had the Great Benefit of making me Aware of what a Phony Federal Government we have, which made me Suspicious of everything that comes Out of Washington, District of Chief Criminals. Therefore, I do not Object to the Lessons that I Learned by going to Vietnam, which Lessons were also Learned by many Veterans of all Wars, who will Naturally Agree with me — that is, except for those Poor Souls who were "Soaked" in Capitalist Propagandist LIES, whereby they are still Pledging their Allegiance to that Bloody Rag, which Represents the Synagogue of Satan, which Permits more than 84,000 Harmful Chemicals to be Sold and Used by Unsuspecting Victims of Capitalism, who are Sure that the Good Drug and Bad Food Administration (FDA) would never Allow anything Harmful to be Sold in America: beCause the Fatherly Federal Government is Watching Out for us Education Slaves, Work Slaves, Tax Slaves, Interest Slaves, Insurance Slaves, Drug Slaves, Rent Slaves, Childcare Slaves and Endless Bills Slaves. †§‡§§

11-02 [_] So, O Selected King of **The Worldwide People's Revolution!®**, it is Obvious that you only needed to be "Burned" just one Time, in Order for you to Learn your Lessons, huh?

11-03 [_] Well, Actually, to be Perfectly Honest with you, I had to Learn a few Hard Lessons long before I got into the Army, beginning in the Fifth Grade in the Public School of Ignorant Fools, when I nearly got my Neck Broken during what they called a "Dog Pile," whereby a half dozen or more Children jumped on my Back, while I was bent over on the Ground, whereby my Head got under my own Body, which came close to Killing me: beCause a couple of those Boys weighed no less than 200 Pounds, each, while I might have weighted 75 Pounds. However, as if that was not Bad enough, I was Riding a Young Stud Horse, Bareback, during the previous Summer, when I was 10 Years Old, and the Horse was Running Full Speed, when he Suddenly came to a STOP, and I went Flying over his Head, and Landed on my own Head, which, once again, nearly Broke my Neck, and probably would have, if it had not been for the Fact that I had been doing a lot of

Work, Feeding and Watering 200 Hogs, 40 Cattle, and whatever else on our Dad's Ranch, in Montana, which Strengthened my Muscles. I also did a lot of "Pull Ups" and "Push Ups": beCause I always liked Big Muscles, ever since I saw one of those Billboards along the Highway, whereby I was just Naturally Magnetized to them: beCause of the Beauty of all such Muscles, as well as Healthy Blond and Bronze Skin. Therefore, when I got into the Army, I was in Good Physical Shape, and had no Trouble with their Exercises, since I could do 300 Pushups within 30 Minutes. {NOTE: Even at 72 Years of Age, I can still do 100 Consecutive Non-stop Push Ups, and as many as 1,000 within an Hour, if the Weather is Cool, which is not Bad for an Old Man, I would say, since I am not a Body Builder of any Kind, nor have I ever been; but, I have done a HUGE Amount of Difficult Work. For the Proof, see: **"What is WRong with those CRAZY Christians?" (A Self-Examination of the Heart of the Body of Good Government!) By The Worldwide People's Revolution!®**, Book 076, plus: **"LIGHTNING STRIKES Versus Lightning Bugs and Impotent Fireflies!" (A Memorial Photo Album of some Real American Heroes!) By The Worldwide People's Revolution!®**, Book 072, which is a Companion Book of: **"The BEST of CAPITALISM!" (Corrections for: LIGHTNING STRIKES Versus Lightning Bugs and Impotent Fireflies!) By The Worldwide People's Revolution!®** Book 073. Both Books contain more than 100 Photographs with Explanations, if I Remember Correctly. I had to Delete the Books from my Computer, which was Crashed by those Photographs: beCause of being Overloaded in Word for Windows, or something else. I have never Learned just WHY; but, I put the Blame onto Capitalism. Moreover, I Lost thousands of Photographs for the same Reason, and I do not know that I will ever be Able to Recover them. Therefore, I have little Respect for such a False System. I can hardly wait for the Establishment of **"The New RIGHTEOUS One-World Government!" (HOW to Establish a Righteous One-World Government without Going to WAR!) By The Worldwide People's Revolution!®** Book 056.}

11-04 [_] So, O Elected King of **"The New RIGHTEOUS One-World Government,"** without going into any Gory Details, did you Discover the GLORIES of War? *"Oh say, can you still See that Bloody Star-spangled Banner yet Waving over the Home of the Spiritually Dead Work Slaves, Tax Slaves, Insurance Slaves and Interest Slaves?"* †§‡

11-05 [_] Well, I would not Refer to the Horrors of Wars as "Glories," even though the Governments of the Worlds have most often Referred to those Gory Wars as Glorious Events with Great Victories — such as the Bloody American Revolutionary War, whereby one-third of George Washington's Army was made up of Black Slaves, who would likely all Agree with me that there is nothing Glorious about any such Wars. However, when a Great Swanky Army of WORKING Soldiers get one of those First Class Swanky Fortresses Finished, they will have something to be very PROUD of, you might say, even though it is Better to just Thank God for having the Building Materials, Proper Tools to Work with, and the Strength and Abilities to get it all done: beCause we could have all been Born Blind and/or Deaf, whereby it would have been much more Difficult to Accomplish anything, much less be Able to Appreciate the Great Beauty of it all, if were Blind, like some of those Professing "Christians," who often say: "I have no Interest in Helping to Build any of those Swanky Palaces: because I am going to Heaven when I Die, to Live in the New Jerusalem, which is the Mightiest Swanky Fortress of all! Besides that, GOD is my Mighty Fortress, who will Protect me from those Hydrogen Bombs, just like he Protected the Japanese Women and Children in Hiroshima and Nagasaki, when the Atomic Bombs fell on them. And I am not Deceived nor Crazy by any Means: beCause I am Born Again. Halleluiah!" †§‡§§

11-06 [_] So, will the Working Soldiers get to Live within the same Fortress that they Build; or, will they Complete only PART of a Project, and then Move on to another Project? For Example, it Requires a lot of TIME to Learn any certain Skill — such as Tile Setting. Therefore, it would be a Great Shame to Learn that Skill, and then not go on Using it, until all of the Swanky Fortresses are Finished. †‡

11-07 [_] Well, that brings up an Interesting Subject, which should be Decided at: **"The Great Worldwide TELEVISED Court HEARING!" (That Great Meeting of the Most Intelligent and Well-Educated Minds!) By The Worldwide People's Revolution!®** Book 041. After all, there are about 7 Billion People in this World of Wonders, who will likely Want to Build their own Private Swanky Fortresses, and also OWN them, Personally, whereby they can Order their Millions of Slaves to do the Dirty Work for them: beCause it is Impossible for a single Family to Attend to all of the House Cleaning and Gardening at a Swanky Fortress; but, it is not at all Impossible for a Billion or more People to Attend to all such Things, and thus get to ENJOY their **"GLORIOUS Swanky Hotels Castles and Fortresses!" (Beautiful Planned City States for WISE Intelligent Well-Educated People with Common Sense and Good Understanding!) By The Worldwide People's Revolution!®**, Book 019, which will Raise their Standards of Living by at least a hundred Times, if not by 10,000 Times! After all, there are more than 5,000 Advantages for Building and Living within all such Swanky Fortresses, for which most Ignorant People never Stop to THINK about it: beCause they are Spiritual BABIES, and Mentally SICK Babies, who just Ignore the BILLIONS of Suffering Peoples in this World of Woes, while Hoping to God that they do not become like them! However, God said that we should Love our Naaberz just as much as we Love ourselves, which Means that we would Want to Raise their Standards of Living by at least a hundred Times, just to have Good Consciences, after Wasting 50% or more of the Natural Resources of Gases, Oils, Coals, Metals, Minerals, Rare Trees, and other Precious Resources, most of which have ended up in Selfish GREEDY Capitalist TRASH DUMPS! Yes, be Sure to HIDE that Trash from your Eyeballs, O Capitalists: beCause it is Embarrassingly Disgraceful for Educated People, who Proclaim themselves to be "Christians," to be Ignoring almost all of the Teachings of Jesus Christ, who would most Certainly NOT Object to the Construction of those **"Beautiful Swanky PALACES!" (A New Concept in Living Habits — Swanky Palaces for Poor People!) By The Worldwide People's Revolution!®**, Book 066: beCause he was a Man of LOVE, MERCY, and COMPASSION, who would much rather See **"Seven Great Armies of Working Soldiers!" (HOW to Provide a Way for Everyone to WORK: so as to Eliminate Poverty, Crimes, Drug Abuses, Prisons and Unnecessary Taxes!) By The Worldwide People's Revolution!®**, Book, 015, Exercising their Beautiful Muscles on something Extra Beautiful and Constructive, than Wasting his Natural Resources on their PRIDE and FOOLISHNESS, while putting themselves in DANGER of a Great Atomic NIGHTMARE! — and all for the LACK of **"The New RIGHTEOUS One-World Government!" (HOW to Establish a Righteous One-World Government without Going to WAR!) By The Worldwide People's Revolution!®** Book 056. However, if anyone Disagrees with me, I Pray to God that they get their Just Reward when the Big Bombs FALL ON THEM! YES, may their Eyeballs MELT in their Sockets, and their Lying Deceiving Tongues FALL OUT! But, Understand that it will not be MY FAULT: beCause I have done my Best to Educate them and Enlighten their Minds with my Inspired Words of Provable Truths! Yes, it will be the Fault of their own UNBELIEF, Stubbornness, SELFISHNESS, Ignorance, and GREED! Moreover, you can Print up Copies of this Page, and pass them out to whomever might have an Open Hand or Heart, who can Discover those Books and many more on the Internet, at: www.Amazon.com / usa. May God Bless you for it.

11-08 [_] So, are you saying that you have not Figured Out the Best Solution for that "Problem," which becomes a Problem, later on, after People Move Into all such Beautiful "Planned" City States, only to Discover that some Less-than-Artistic Working Soldiers did not *Do with all of their Might whatsoever their Hands Found to Do."* (See *Ecclesiastes 9:10; and First Chronicles 28:20.*)

11-09 [_] Well, Ideally, each Family would Build their own House as they might be Pleased to do it. However, not one Man in a thousand would have any Idea concerning just HOW to Build the Pantheon, in Rome, for Example. Perhaps it is Best if the Working Soldiers get everything Finished, except for Tiling the Walls, which can be done by each Family — except that a Professional Well-Trained Tile Setter would Naturally do a much Better Job than the Normal Inexperienced Person.

11-10 [_] So, the Bottom Line is this: The Citizens of each Beautiful Planned City State must Decide for themselves just HOW to Build their own Ideal Places to Live, and be Totally Responsible for HOW it gets Done, huh? {See www.Amazon.com for: **"The IDEAL Place to Live!" (HOW to Discover the Ideal Place to Live!) By The Worldwide People's Revolution!®** Book 069.} In other Words, each Person must Fill Out and File: **"The Complete SURVEYS of our VALUES!" (SURVEYS of Religious Spiritual Political Governmental Sexual Social Moral Economic Business Labor Habitual and Miscellaneous VALUES!),** whereby it can be Determined WHERE and with WHOM all such People should Live and Work with other People of Like-mindedness: so that they can all be Happy with one another, even as Sheeps are Happy to Live with other Sheeps, and Wolves are Happy to Live with other Wolves, "and thus not be Arguing over which Color to Paint the Pews in the Unholy Church of Graceful Sinners on the Corner of Lonesome Street and Suicide Avenue," as Tom Sawyer might say to Huck Finn and Nigger Jim, if he knows for Sure that his Aunt Polly is not Listening, while Hiding in the Closet of Forgetfulness with Hilarious Rotten Clinton and/or Donald Jaywalking Lying Trumpeter with his 5,000+ Naked Security Guards, who Carry Radioactive Isotopes in their most Quiet Top Secret Diamond-studded "Christian" Sneakers, if ye knoweth what I Means, as Nigger Jim might say to Raggedy Ann Huck Finn, according to the Interpretation of the Low Court of Supreme Injustices, who have their own Private Interpretation of *Freedom of Speech,* which they say is MONEY! {See: **"Mark Twain Races for the PRESIDENCY!" (The 2020 Presidential Candidates Desperately Need some STRONG Undefeatable COMPETITION!) By The Worldwide People's Revolution!®** Book 033. Please Check the following Boxes [_] with X Marks, if you Agree with the Statements. Thank you.}

> A-[_] I Agree that the one and only Riit Waa to Discover the IDEAL House and City to Build for Good Living, is to DEMAND **"The Great Worldwide TELEVISED Court HEARING,"** whereby we might Learn the Best Plan, whereby we might Save the most Time, Money, Materials, and Energy in the Construction of all such Houses and Cities: beCause some People might have Special Nolij that we should all Learn. After all, the Riit Plan might Save us Earthlings Millions of Trillions of Dollars! ‡

> B-[_] It is my Firm Belief that our Selected King already has the Best Master Plan. However, I do not Object to Hearing any other Plans, if someone Imagines that he or she has Better Plans. In Fact, I am Curious if anyone else on the Whole Earth has even Thought about it, after Considering the Fact that I have never Heard any Politician, Preacher nor

Teacher Talk about it; nor do I Expect to Hear them Talking about it in a Positive Way: beCause they would Vainly Imagine that they would have to Borrow the Necessary Money from the Edomite Bankers for Building those Trillion-Dollar Planned City States, which is simply NOT True: beCause a RIGHTEOUS Government has no Need for any Bankers, at all, which can easily be Proven in a Courtroom with Law and Order! ‡ {See: **"Are we Tax Slaves of a Lower Order than those Lying (Conniving) EDOMITES?" (HOW to be Liberated from all Slavery, Worldwide!) By The Worldwide People's Revolution!®** Book 052.}

C-[_] I Confess that all such Subjects are far too Deep and Mysterious for me to Understand: beCause I have a very Shallow Mind, which Contemplates Suicide much of the Time: beCause I am Totally Confounded by the FACTS. Indeed, I would Like to get RID of all of my Bills; but, I cannot Visualize any Way to Do it, and still be a Proud Property Owner, which is a Necessity of LIFE, at least for me: beCause I must OWN the Air that I Breathe, the Mountains that I See, the Sunrises and Sunsets, the Forests in the Amazon Basin, the Oceans, the Rivers, the Lakes, the Water that I Drink, and the Foods that I Eat: beCause I was Created in the Image of GOD, whose Chosen Son said: *Take no Thoughts for your Life — not even for Tomorrow, for what you shall Eat nor Drink nor wherewithal you shall be Clothed: beCause Sufficient unto each Day is the Evil thereof. Is not the Body more Important than Clothing? Is not your Life more Important than Eating? What about your Spirit — how long has it been since your Soul was Satisfied with my Inspired Words of Provable Truths? Indeed, if you are Wise, and Self-Disciplined Disciple, you shall Live like the Birds of the Air, who neither Sow Seeds, nor Gather Grains into Barns and Silos; and yet your Heavenly Father takes Good Care of them, whereby Billions of Birds Die each Winter, and especially when it gets Severely Cold with Deep Snow on the Ground. Nevertheless, you are of much more Value to God than Birds, who should Live by Faith, even as I Live: beCause you are my Disciples. Yes, Consider the Lilies of the Fields, and how they do not Toil nor Spin; and yet they are more Finely Clothed than King Solomon in all of his Naked Glory, who Failed to Explain just HOW the Masses of People should Live, Properly, who should have Formed Seven Great Armies of Working Soldiers, whereby the Israelites might have Built Beautiful Planned City States, which use Elevators, Escalators and Electric Subway Trains: so as to Save hundreds of Trillions of Dollars on Transportation Costs and other Nonsense — such as Insurance, Traffic Tickets, Traffic Jams, Traffic Lights, and Traffic Police, and thus not Pollute the Air, Water nor Land with any Abominations; but, Poor Old King Solomon never Thought of it, in spite of being a Seer, who Supposedly Saw every Event of the Past, Present and Future, according to the Unholy Mutilated Bible, which does not even Mention any Beautiful Planned City States, except for the Ridiculous New Jerusalem, in the Book of Revelation, which is supposedly 1,500 Miles Tall, being mostly Out of the Atmosphere, which Cities must be Designed for LIVING! And Proper Living would Begin with Fresh Clean AIR, Pure Living Water, Wholesome Natural Foods, Proper Natural Clothing, and SECURE Bomb-proof Self-air-conditioned Fireproof Tornado-proof Hurricane-proof Earthquake-proof Mouse-proof Termite-proof Rot-proof Paint-proof Insurance-proof HOUSES, like the Pantheon in Rome, within Beautiful Planned City States for WISE Intelligent Well-Educated People with Common Sense and Good Understanding! Yes, all such Cities should be Designed for Eternal Employment at Home, having Home-craft Workshops, Sales Shops, Spacious Kitchens, Storage Rooms, Ice Houses, Walk-in Coolers, Large Cisterns for Water Storage, and Especially LARGE All-Mineral Organic Gardens, whereby the Families can Feed themselves the Best Living Foods in the World, whereby they will not have any Need for the very Expensive Services of the Doctor Knife, Doctor Pill Popper, Doctor Puss Shooter, nor Doctor Insanity. Therefore, Seek First the Good Government of the Gods, and then all of those Necessities of Life will be Added unto you, O Ignorant Fools, and without any Endless Bills to Pay, O Deceived Slaves!" — The New Beggar's Version of Matthew 6:25— 34 in Plain English for Honest People, who do not Suffer with Chronic Constipation of their Minds!* †§‡§§

D-[ ] Damned if I will Accept any such Satanic Words, which did not come from my Holy Bible. CURSED is the Man who Teaches any other Gospel than the one that is Taught by the Reformed Church of Pentecostal Methodists of the Seventh-day Southern Baptist Convention of Episcopalian Lutherans, who have been Sanctified by the Roman Catholic Brotherhood of the Jesuit Muslims and Hindu Buddhists, who are Dimwitcrats and Reprobates of the First Order of Independent Jackasses, who should Try to Understand that there are more than 200 Mistranslated Versions of the Unholy Mutilated Bible: beCause each Hebrew or Greek Word has 5, 10, 20, 50, or 100 Different Definitions for each Word, even as it is in English, except that Hebrew and Greek Words are less Definitive! For Example, "Earth" or "Erets" in Hebrew means "the whole World" (but, not the Universe) in *Genesis 1:2;* "the Land" in *Genesis 1:10;* a "Country" in *Genesis 21:32;* a "Plot of Ground" in *Genesis 23:15;* "the Ground on which a Man Stands" in *Genesis 33:3;* "the Inhabitants of the Earth" in *Genesis 6:1 and 11:1;* "all of the World, except for Israel" in *Second Chronicles 13:9;* and "the Earth" in the *New Testament* means "the Land of Judea" in *Matthew 23:35;* and "things Carnal" in contrast with "things Heavenly" in *John 3:31 and Colossians 3:1—2. "Love not the World, neither any of the Things in the World,"* is not Referring to the Earth in *First John 2:15. "For God so Loved the World, that he Gave his only Begotten Son ..."* So, you can See that there is Absolutely NO Confusion there. *Strong's Exhaustive Concordance* confesses that "Ehrets" comes from an Unused Root Word, which Probably Means to be "Firm." It was Translated as: land, earth, country, ground, world, way, common, field, nations, and wilderness. As "Land," it could Mean "Country, Territory, District, Region, Tribal Territory, Piece of Ground, Land of Canaan, Israel, Inhabitants of Land, Sheol (Hell), Land without Return, Underworld, World, City, City State, Ground, Soil, Topsoil, Subsoil, People of the Land, Space, Distance to Country, Level or Plain Country, Land of the Living, Land of the Dead, End or Ends of the Earth, Foreign Lands, Countries, Deserts, Stuff, Possessions, and so on. The same Word was used to make some 2,000+ Different Translations in the King James Version and in other Versions — all of which can be Proven to have Ridiculous Errors. Otherwise, there would not be 200+ Contradictory Versions! †§‡§§

E-[ ] Educated People Know for a Fact that our Selected King has the Correct Translations of all such *Scriptures:* beCause he has the Gift of the Holy Spirit, whereby he Wrote the New MAGNIFIED Version (NMV) within less than 3 Years by the Spirit of Inspiration. Moreover, the Holy Spirit Revealed that many so-called *"Scriptures"* were Edomite Additions and Exaggerations, which could not be Properly Translated into any Language without Misleading People — such as the Noah's Ark Edomite Exaggerations, the Samson Edomite Exaggerations, and the King Nebuchadnezzar Edomite Exaggerations. {See:

"The New MAGNIFIED Version of the GOOD NEWS According to Saint LUKE!" (The Magnified Gospel of Luke in Plain English!) By The Worldwide People's Revolution!®, Book 061, which is a Companion Book of: **"The New MAGNIFIED Version of the Book of ACTS!" (The Understandable Version of the ACTS of the Apostles in Plain English!) By The Worldwide People's Revolution!®**, Book 063, which Thoroughly Explains HOW the First Church of Jesus Christ became so Persecuted by the HOLY JEWS, who sought to Utterly Destroy them by all Means Available to them! For Example, they Sent out the Man called SAUL, to Round Up those Christians, and put them to Death. (See *Acts 7,* and *Revelation 2:9 and 3:9, KJV.*) Yes, you Need to EJUKAAT yourself, O Lady Doubtfulness.}

F-[_] I Fail to Understand WHY everyone in the Whole World would not just Cheerfully SUBMIT to our Selected King, and DO whatever he Commands us: beCause he has Clearly Stated that everyone who Objects to his Master Plan is Welcome to Live within our Present-day Cities of Confusion, or on Farms, Ranches, and in Wilderness Resorts, if they are Independent Jackasses, who HATE those **"Beautiful Swanky PALACES!" (A New Concept in Living Habits — Swanky Palaces for Poor People!) By The Worldwide People's Revolution!®** Book 066. Indeed, there will Naturally be X-amount of Rebels, who will not Voluntarily Join any of the **"Seven Great Armies of Working Soldiers!" (HOW to Provide a Way for Everyone to WORK: so as to Eliminate Poverty, Crimes, Drug Abuses, Prisons and Unnecessary Taxes!) By The Worldwide People's Revolution!®**, Book 015, nor even any of: **"The Swanky Associations of Working Soldiers!" (A Fascinating Collection of Various Kinds of Voluntary Working Soldiers!) By The Worldwide People's Revolution!®** Book 018. Therefore, they do not have to be Failures in Life, if they are very Innovative People with Good Imaginations: beCause they will still be FREE to Practice Capitalism, Communism, Socialism, Fascism, or whatever they Like — just as long as they Agree to Live in PEACE, and do not become Terrorists like George Warmonger Bush nor Little Dick Chicanery, Incorporated! †§‡§§

G-[_] God Knows that there is Plenty of Space in this World of Wonders for even Fools, if that is what they Choose to be; but, most of the People will just Naturally and GLADLY Choose to become Moderately RICH, like our Selected King, who OWNS NOTHING but a couple of Used Computers and an Electronic Keyboard for Playing Music, who Lives in a Million-Dollar Mansion; but, nothing so Lavish as the Palaces of the Pope of Rome, who will be Happy to Assist everyone in the Whole World to Obtain far Better Palaces, if they are Willing to Learn and WORK for them. Yes, he will Gladly Host **"The Great Worldwide TELEVISED Court HEARING,"** in Saint Peter's Basilica: beCause it is Designed for that Special Meeting of the Most Intelligent Minds, being Preordained of GOD for that Holy Purpose! {See: **"LIGHTNING STRIKES Versus Lightning Bugs!" (HOW you can Become Moderately RICH, without Telling any Lies nor Selling any Trash!) By The Worldwide People's Revolution!®**, Book 074, which contains many Photos with Explanations for his Modest Harmless Lifestyle.}

H-[_] I Honestly have no Idea what you People are Talking about. Do you come from the Planet Earth, or from some other World?? I have been Taught since Childhood that this World is NOT our Eternal HOME: beCause we are ALL going to HEAVEN when we Die, according to *John 3:13,* and *Psalm 115:16, KJV,* along with Judas Iscariot and Bernie Madoff, who were Typical Edomites, whom the Hebrew God HATED, according to *Romans 9:13,* which is Thoroughly Explained in that Inspired Book, called: **"Are we Tax Slaves of a Lower Order than those Lying EDOMITES?" (HOW to be Liberated from all Slavery, Worldwide!) By The Worldwide People's Revolution!®** Book 052. †§‡§§

I-[_] I am an Innocent Child, who would Like to Retain my Innocence, who has not been Inoculated with any Edomite Propagandist Lies; nor do I Want to be: beCause I can be quite Contented with Fresh Clean Air, Good Natural Wholesome Foods, Good Natural Wholesome Drinks, Natural Clothing, and the Luxuries of those **"Beautiful Swanky PALACES,"** which will have Churches, Theaters, Concert Halls, Gymnasiums, Indoors Heated Swimming Pools, Sauna Baths, Tennis Courts, Bowling Alleys, Game Rooms, **Royal Swanky Buffets**, thousands of Stone Dome Home Complexes, Millions of Fruit Trees, Nut Trees, Grape Vines, Berry Bushes, Vegetable Gardens, Flower Gardens, Waterfalls, HUGE Cisterns for Water Storage, FREE Electric Power, Wide-screen Televisions, Free Computers, Free Pollution-free Transportation, Free Telephone Services, Free Spectacular Waterworks, Free Musical Instruments, Free Books, Free Entertainments, Free Burial Services, and Free Medical Services — all in Exchange for only 4 Hours of Common Skilled Labor per Day, or the Equivalent thereof, Tax-free, Insurance-free, Loan-free, Interest-free, Worry-free, Bedbug-free, Lice-free, Mice-free, Rat-free, Raccoon-free, Opossum-free, Skunk-free, Snake-free, Termite-free, Fire-ant-free, Flea-free, Politician-free, Lying-preacher-free, Wicked-lawyer-free, Unjust-judge-free, Prison-free, Crime-free, Pollution-free, Greasy-car-free, Debt-free, Traffic-jam-free, Car-accident-free, Crippled-Victims of Capitalism-free, and so on — even a whole List of FREEDOMS that we do not presently have: beCause of Losing our INNOCENCE, O Fools! †§‡§§

J-[_] Justice Demands that King Jesus must Return, in Order to have all of those Freedoms, Liberty, and Justice for ALL! †§‡

K-[_] King Jesus has already Arrived, and I am going to VOTE for him! Yes, we will make him our Powerless President, who will not be Able to Do anything without the Approval of the CONgress, and of the Lower Courts of Supreme Injustices, who should be brought to Trial for Ignoring the Inspired Books of our Selected King. †§‡§§

L-[_] Lots of Laughs! King Jesus will not even Think about Returning, until we have Constructed **"The Great World TEMPLE of PEACE"** for him; but, NOT in Jerusalem: beCause it is already Covered up with Ugly Old Buildings, which would only Inspire the Religious Idiots to go to WAR, if we should Touch them. Therefore, we must Build that Great Temple in the Spacious State of Flexible TEXAS! Yes, there is Plenty of Space for it and many of those **"GLORIOUS Swanky Hotels Castles and Fortresses"** surrounding it, all of the Way into Mexico and Montana: beCause God has Reserved those Wide-open Spaces for such an Hour as this, when the Liberty Bells can Ring Out FREEDOM with a Capital F; and the Prison Doors can all be Opened to whomever is Willing to REPENT! See: **"The Proper RULES for FASTING!" (The Complete Instruction Manual for True Repentance!) By The Worldwide People's Revolution!®**, Book 046, which is a Companion Book of: **"HOW to Become a HOLY Man!" (40 Good Reasons WHY**

People Should FAST and PRAY!) By The Worldwide People's Revolution!® Book 045. Yes, what a GLORIOUS Day that will be, when Jesus Sees that we are Actually Practicing his True Teachings, whereby he will begin to Think about Returning in all of his Naked Glory, being about 400 Miles TALL, whereby every Eye can See him, according to *Revelation 1:7, KJV.* Yes, just that Fact of Life will Require it: beCause, if he were NOT at least 400 Miles Tall, HOW would the People in Honduras get to See him Riding his Great White Horse in the Sky over New York City, as he Circles the Earth at 4,000 Miles per Hour with the Lunar Landing Module of the Saturn V Rocket at his Horse's Tail? Truly, Truly, I say unto thee, such a Silly Thing is IMPOSSIBLE, O LADY Doubtfulness. †§‡§§

M-[_] MONEY is the one and only Solution in this Case, which will Require Lots and LOTS of it: beCause those **"GLORIOUS Swanky Hotels Castles and Fortresses"** will Cost MILLIONS of TRILLIONS of Dollars: beCause each Toilet and Bathroom Sink will have to be Covered with Pure GOLD, just to make People like Donald Jaywalking Trumpeter HAPPY! Otherwise, he will be Speaking EVIL of those Swanky Fortresses! Therefore, we will have to Haul OUT all of the Gold within those Edomite Bank Vaults, and Use it WISELY to Decorate our Theaters, Churches, Mosques, Synagogues, Temples, Cathedrals, Auditoriums, Concert Halls, **Royal Swanky Buffets**, Restaurants, Tables, Dining Room Chairs, Mirrors, and whatever else with Diamond-studded Decorations that will make Donald Jaywalking Trumpeter Greatly Ashamed of himself. Meanwhile, the Baby Jesus will be Born in another Manger, East of Eden, somewhere around the Middle East, if we can Find it and him, who will have to be Reincarnated: beCause there is no such a Thing as a Resurrection, even if the Mormons Believe it. See www.Amazon.com for: **"The New MAGNIFIED Version of The Book of MORMON!" (The Story of the White and Dark Indians in the Americas!) By The Worldwide People's Revolution!**® Books 040-A and 040-B. †§‡§§

N-[_] Not everyone is High on Drugs, like you, O Nightingale of Shakespearian Religious Dreams. First of all, if there is no Resurrection of the Dead, our Hope in Jesus Christ is all in VAIN: beCause we are all Bound to DIE, sooner or later. Therefore, we must have a Nostalgic Hope in a Resurrection of some Kind, even if Donald Jumping Jacks is left Behind: beCause no such Liar is Worthy of any such Resurrection, which you are Welcome to DENY; but, there are many *Scriptures* to Prove it, from *Noah and Nehemiah* to *Mark Anthony and Jonah the Whale, the Son of Saint Nicolas the Third.* †§‡§§ (See: *Revelation 5:10; 20:5—6; 22:15; First Thessalonians 4:16—18; Matthew 12:18—; 22:30—; 27:53; Luke 14:14; 20:27—;* **20:35; John 5:29,** *Acts 1:22; 2:31; 4:33; 17:18, 32; 23:8; 24:15; First Corinthians 15:12—; Second Timothy 2:18—; Hebrews 6:2; 11:35; First Peter 1:3, KJV.* †§‡

O-[_] It is my Honest Opinion that Crazy Religious People should be Separated from the Sane People, which will be easy to Do by having everyone Fill Out and File **"The Complete SURVEYS of our VALUES!" (SURVEYS of Religious Spiritual Political Governmental Sexual Social Moral Economic Business Labor Habitual and Miscellaneous VALUES!) By The Worldwide People's Revolution!**® Book 059. Therefore, everyone will have a Multitude of OPTIONS to Choose from, just by Checking the Appropriate Boxes in the Surveys, after Studying the Statements Carefully with Open

Minds and Sincere Hearts. For Example, I Opt Out of the Swanky Associations of Pumpkinheads, who Believe in a Rapture of the Church. †§‡ {See www.Amazon.com for: **"The PRAYERS of PUMPKINHEADS!" (Even God Needs a little Humor to Cheer himself Up!) By The Worldwide People's Revolution!® Book 007.**}

P-[_] Persistent People like you should come Down from Cloud 9, and get yourself into a Real World, since no one on the Earth has enough Time to Study all such Crazy Books, unless they have Retired in some Old People's Rest Home on Crank Street and Pimpledicker Avenue, after Drinking Pesticides for the Past 60 or so Years, whereby they Suffer with Paralysis of the Pituitary Gland. †§‡ {See: **"The Seven Basic Spiritual Building Blocks of LIFE!" (Faith Hope Trust Love Patience Persistence and Obedience!) By The Worldwide People's Revolution!®**, Book 036, which is a Companion Book of: **"SWANGKEENOMIKS Rules the Roost!" (HOW all People can Prosper in a RIIT WAA, and STOP Polluting the Earth with Capitalist TRASH!) By The Worldwide People's Revolution!® Book 039.**}

Q-[_] The Great Question is this: **"Should People be Free to Choose the Kinds of Trash Dumps that they Want to Live in; or, should they simply be HIRED to Help Build Beautiful Planned City States for themselves to Live in, whereby they would soon Discover that they are Free, Healthy, and HAPPY, even as Young Voluntary Working SOLDIERS, who would never Want to Leave any such Beautiful Swanky PALACES with the Marble-faced Walls, Granite-faced Floors, Agate Windows, and Polished Onyx Tables?"** Indeed, you could not Drag them Away from any such Glorious Places, to go Live in some Filthy Noisy Dangerous Trash Dump like the South Side of Chicago, or the Slums of Sao Paulo, Brazil; or the Filth and Squalor of Calcutta, India. †§‡ {See: **"A Sure Cure for GUN VIOLENCE!" (HOW TO STOP GANG WARS and CRIMINAL SHOOTINGS!) By The Worldwide People's Revolution!® Book 031.**}

R-[_] Resurrection or no Resurrection, I am a Convert! Indeed, I Sincerely Believe that I will be Reincarnated in the Body of a Muslim, if I do not Accept Christian Doctrines — such as Baptisms for the Dead, which only one Church on the Earth even Believes in: beCause they have more Faith in Living by every Word that Proceeds out of the Mouth of the Gods — such as Allah God, Jehovah God, Yahweh God, Hairy Krishna's God, Buddha's God, and any of those other Gods, whom I have yet to Meet in **"The BIG White OUTHOUSE on the Not-so-Biblical Capitol DUNGHILL!"** Book 023. However, I have a HOPE to Meet at least one of those Gods when my Judgment Day comes, whereby I might Ask him or her a few Important Questions — such as, "Why did you not Send that Colorful Peacock from Angel Ridge to us about a hundred Years Ago, whereby we might have had some Time to Think about all such Inspired Words of Provable Truths, whereby we might have Avoided a hundred Years of Needless Sufferings?" And then God will Naturally Respond with something like this: *"Are you Sure that you have now Suffered Long Enough to come to your Right Senses with the Prodigal Son of Luke 15?"* †§‡§§

S-[_] Saint Stephen would be Happy to See this Extremely Stupid Generation, whereby he could say with a Good Conscience: *"Father, please Forgive them: beCause they do not Realize what they are Doing to themselves."* Indeed, if they had any Common Sense, at all, they would be DEMANDING **"The Great Worldwide TELEVISED Court HEARING,"** whereby they might Discover whether or not there is a God of JUSTICE, who would Surely not Leave us in the Darkness of Ignorance FOREVER! However, Stupid People hardly Deserve to See the Light of Provable Truths, whereby they might be Liberated from their Unsanitary Prisons of Outlandish Lies! Yes, may they Wash their Faces with Recycled Sewage Water, instead of Pure Living Water within Swanky Fortresses, which is Kept Fresh at all Times: beCause of Pumping it from Lower Cisterns up to Higher Cisterns, whereby it can be used Wisely for making Beautiful Waterfalls throughout the Swanky Fortresses, which is otherwise known as Natural Music, which, when Combined with the Music of Beautiful Birds Chirping, among Trees that are Loaded with Sweet Ripe Fruits, it will be one of the most Pleasantest Things that one ever Heard and Seen, which will be Greatly Enhanced by the Stonework of the many Swanky Terraces, which will also be Admired by the Holy Angels, who will just Naturally come to Visit the Children of GOD, who will have a New SONG to Sing during those Wonderful Days! †§‡

T-[ ] It is now Time to Publish this Good News, Worldwide, and in all Major Languages, whereby everyone can Learn about it, and all of the Young People can Join **The Worldwide People's Revolution!®** Yes, they can Dress themselves in their most Colorful Costumes, even as the Members of **"Seven Great Swanky Armies of Voluntary Working Soldiers!"** who will just Naturally Glum on to each other like Elmer's Glue Sticks to Dry Paper, and nothing on the Earth will be Able to Separate them from the LOVE of ALL that is GOOD! May the Gods Help you to See the Wonderful Vision of it, O Lady Doubtfulness! May the Wind be at your Back, and the Golden Slippers on your Feet, O Saint Jeffrey Preston Bezos: beCause, what Better Thing on this Earth could you Do, than to put a Copy of this Inspired Book in every Mailbox in **"The Divided States of United Lies!" (The so-called "United States of North America" in Disguise!) By The Worldwide People's Revolution!®**, Book 058? Indeed, they Desperately Need some INSPIRATION, which is not likely to come from the Swamp in Washington, District of Chief Criminals: beCause they have their Heads STUCK in those 2 Stinking Holes in **"The BIG White OUTHOUSE on the Not-so-Biblical Capitol DUNGHILL!"** Book 023. †§‡

U-[ ] I Understand what you are Saying, and it is altogether True; but, what if most Americans Reject this Book on Account of their Great Unbelief? Indeed, suppose they Boycott my Businesses, and Burn Down my Houses — where will I go for Refuge?

V-[ ] Well, my Friend, your Important Question is Answered by the Apostle Paul, who wrote: *"Yes, and all who desire to live godly in Christ Jesus will suffer persecution. But evil men and impostors will grow worse and worse, deceiving and being deceived. But you must continue in the things which you have learned and been assured of, knowing from whom you have learned them, and that from childhood you have known the Holy Scriptures, which are able to make you wise for salvation through faith which is in Christ Jesus." — Second Timothy 3:12—15, NKJV.* Yes, I will now Quote it to you from the New MAGNIFIED Version — *"Yes, and all People who Desire to Live Godly Lives, according to the Teachings of Jesus Christ, will Suffer Persecutions; but, Understand this, that Evil Men and Impostors will Grow Worse and WORSE, Deceiving and being Deceived: beCause of the Love of Money, which is the Root Cause for almost all Evils: beCause*

Capitalism, for Example, has no Conscience, no Morality, no Empathy for Poor Miserable Souls, and no Compassion for anyone: beCause its Primary Goal is to Minimize Expenses, while Maximizing Profits, whereby it Pays Minimum Wages for Maximum Labor. But, you must be Wise, and Continue Living according to the Good Things that you have Learned and been Assured of, Knowing from whom you have Learned them, and from whom your Blessings have come, and that from Childhood you have Known the Holy Scriptures, which are able to make you Wise for Salvation from all of your Problems, through Faith, which is in Christ Jesus, who was a Holy Man of the Greatest Faith, who did all Kinds of Miracles to Encourage us to have more Faith in his Inspired Words of Provable Truths. Indeed, all Scriptures are given by the Inspiration of God, and are Profitable for Teaching Good Doctrines, for Reproving Sinners, for Correcting the Saints, and for Instructions in the Ways of Righteousness: so that the Man of God might be Perfected, being Thoroughly Furnished with the Correct Tools for every Good Work." Therefore, be it unto you according to your Faith in All that is GOOD. Yes, the VICTORY will be to him who has Faith in God and Goodness. After all, *"What would it Profit a Man, if he should Gain the Whole World, and Lose his Reward in the Kingdom of God?"* Trust me, it is Worth the Sacrifice, which will only Cost about 1 Billion 500 Million Dollars, and might Generate 100 Billion Dollars for your own Bank Account: beCause of Selling 85 or more Inspired Books to each Intelligent American. After all, no one has Better Books to Sell, which you can Prove to yourself by Reading a few of them, which are likely to be more Popular in Foreign Nations: beCause they are less Guilty of American Crimes. †‡

W-[_] It might Cause World War 3 to break out! After all, you are Proposing to Eliminate all Bankers, Insurance Agencies, Paint Factories, Harmful Chemical Corporations, Car Manufacturers, Synthetic Perfume Companies, Weapons Manufacturers, Oil Industries, Gas Companies, Drug Producers, and Non-Organic Farmers, who will not Appreciate such Actions, who will be Ready to go to WAR, just as soon as they Hear about it! †§‡

X-[_] X-amount of Billions of People will be Thanking you for "Eternity" for Helping them to See the Light, including those Intelligent Bankers, Educated Lawyers, Honest Politicians, Compassionate Medical Doctors, Rational Scientists, Construction Workers, Good Cooks, and Honest Businesspeople. Therefore, do not Worry yourself over them: beCause they will eventually Humbly Submit to **"The Swanky Sword of Divine Truths!" (The Most Powerful Weapon in the Whole Universe!) By The Worldwide People's Revolution!® Book 067.**

Y-[_] I am Yearning for the Day when I can go to my Mailbox and Discover ALL of the Inspired Books by our Selected King, even in Hand-carved Leather-bound Editions! Yes, that be **"The END of CONFUSION!" (The Great CELEBRATION of the Magnificent Wedding of the Most Humble Honest Nations, and the Grand Year of JUBILEE!) By The Worldwide People's Revolution!® Book 050.**

Z-[_] The ZEAL of **The Worldwide People's Revolution!®** will make that Possible! (See *Stan Jones — The Spill,* on the C-SPAN TV Network for Saturday, July 21, 2018, for some much-needed Education about Heatless Capitalism.)

— Chapter 12 —

Good Working Soldiers Do GOOD Works!

12-01 [_] Just Imagine what Kind of a BIG MESS that Working Soldiers could Produce, if they were Ordered to Construct Things like the Boston "BIG DIG," which is a 3.5-mile- (5.6 km)- long Artery/Tunnel Project in Boston, Massachusetts, which was the most Expensive Highway Project in the United States of America, from 1991—2007. It was Planned to Cost 2.8 Billion Dollars in 1982 dollars, or 6 Billion by 2006, to adjust for Inflation Costs on the Almighty Dollar. However, the Project was completed at a Cost of 14.6 Billion Dollars for only 3.5 Miles of an Interstate Highway! However, the Money was Naturally Borrowed from those Friendly Bankers, and the Loan will not be Paid Off until 2038, whereby the Total Cost for the Interest and Principle will be an Estimated 22 Billion Dollars! Now, just Think about that for a Minute or 2. Try to Imagine what YOU could Do with 22 Billion Dollars! Well, you could Buy 4,400,000,000 Marble Tiles at 5$ each, which would be enough Tiles to Tile the Walls of 220,000 Houses with about 10 large Rooms, each! Moreover, as of 2015, there are about 590,000 People in Boston, which we can round off at 600,000, and say that there is an Average of 4 People now Living in each House. Therefore, 600,000 divided by 4, equals 150,000 Houses, which could have all been Tiled with Paint-proof Fireproof Marble on the Inside Walls for LESS Money than the Cost of the "Big Dig"! However, if the People of Massachusetts had been at all Wise, they could have simply Claimed their own Rocks, and thus Produced those Mable Tiles for less than 50 Cents, each! However, if they had any Shortage of Rocks in Massachusetts, they could likely Persuade their Sister State, Vermont, to Share some of their Rocks with them, in Exchange for Sharing some Rock Cutting and Polishing Machines with Vermont, whereby they could all have had Marble-faced Walls and Granite-faced Floors, at Cost, which might have been less than one Dollar per Tile, Installed, and for much less Money than the Cost of the "Big Dig"! Yes, all of the People in Vermont and Massachusetts could have Built **"Beautiful Swanky PALACES"** for themselves for a Lower Cost than the "Big Dig," if they had just all VOLUNTEERED to do the Work, while being Fed by "The Garden State," which is New Jersey, which Lacks those Mountains of Rocks, which Vermont could Share with them, just for Feeding the Volunteers, which would only Require about 10% of the People in all of those States: beCause of being Organized like a COORDINATED ARMY of WORKING SOLDIERS! †‡

12-02 [_] So, O Elected King, are you saying that it was Actually Possible for all of the People in Massachusetts, Vermont, and New Jersey to have gotten Together and Organized themselves, and used that 22 Billion Dollars WISELY, and thus made the Necessary Tools for Moving some Rocks around, whereby they could have Built **"Beautiful Swanky PALACES"** for themselves, whereby they could have all become Moderately RICH, just by their Labors, alone — and all for the Price of a Highway that is only 3.5 Miles Long, and does nothing for the People of Vermont, New Jersey, nor Pennsylvania, who could have Produced the Steel and Tools for the other Volunteers to Work with, whereby the People of Pennsylvania could have also been Living in Swanky Palaces, by now, just for being Generous with their Steel? Indeed, are you saying that North Dakota could have Shared some of their Oil and Gas with the Volunteers of Vermont, Massachusetts, New

Jersey, and Pennsylvania, whereby those same Armies of Voluntary Working Soldiers could have also Built Swanky Palaces for all of the People in North Dakota, for their Appreciation of the Generosity of the Kindhearted People of North Dakota, who Willingly Chose to DONATE their Oil and Gas, rather than Sell it for next to nothing to Rich Oil Tycoons in Texas, who Raked in no less than 40 Billion Dollars in PROFITS, just last Year, while Poor Old Mrs. Cripples could not even Afford to Buy a Head of Organically-grown Broccoli for 5$: beCause of Wasting her Money on Expensive Gasoline? Are you saying that all of the Citizens of Texas could have also been Living in **"Beautiful Swanky PALACES,"** if they had not Allowed those Rich Oil Tycoons to Collect 40 Billion Dollars for doing almost nothing, who could have been Selling Gasoline for only 17 Cents per Gallon, like it is now Selling in Venezuela, in South America: beCause of NATIONALIZING the Oil and Gas Companies!? Yes, that is the Truth — a Gallon of Gas in Venezuela is only 17 CENTS, while it is about 4$ per Gallon in Californicate, in **"The Divided States of United Lies!" (The so-called "United States of North America" in Disguise!)**, Book 058! †‡

12-03 [_] Well, I am saying that you Silly People in Boston have been Raped, Robbed, Castrated, and Murdered without even knowing it. Indeed, the Average Bostonian Family Wastes 4 to 6 thousand Dollars, Annually, on Heating and Cooling Bills, depending on the Weather Conditions, which adds up to about 600 to 900 Million Dollars, while I Spend ZERO Dollars on Heating and Cooling Bills: beCause of Acting WISELY. Therefore, why do you Silly People not Wake Up and Use your Heads to THINK? Indeed, if the Walls of your House were 10 feet THICK, you too could have FREE Heating and Cooling, just by Controlling the Windows and Doors, which could be Set Up to Automatically Control themselves! Therefore, you could Save no less than 60 to 90 Billion Dollars within 100 Years — that is, IF there were no INFLATION, whereby those Heating and Cooling Bills might be 60,000$ per Household within 100 Years! †‡

12-04 [_] O Selected King of **The Worldwide People's Revolution!®**, I find it Interesting that the Russians Wasted 52 Billion Dollars on the Winter Olympics, which they could have Used Wisely for Building **"Beautiful Swanky PALACES"** for themselves, whereby X-amount of Poor Russians could have become Moderately Rich. So, WHY is it that there is never any Shortage of Money for Foolishness, such as those Olympic Games; but, no Money for the Necessary TOOLS for Assisting all Poor People to Prosper?

12-05 [_] Well, it is the Nature of Capitalism, which is the Goddess of the Military Industrial Congressional Bankers' Drug Cartel False News Media COMPLEX, whereby X-amount of Rich People can always get Richer, while Poor People get Poorer and Poorer: beCause there is no Righteous KING in Charge of Things! Yes, it is just that Simple, my Friend. {See: **"Are Americans the Most STUPID People who ever Lived?" (HOW Working People can PROSPER and Live in PEACE Under the Rulership of a RIGHTEOUS KING!)**, Book 047, plus: **"The Nature of CAPITALISM!" (A List of the EVILS of CAPITALISM!)**, Book 038, plus: **"Beautiful Swanky PALACES!" (A New Concept in Living Habits — Swanky Palaces for Poor People!) By The Worldwide People's Revolution!®** Book 066.}

12-06 [_] So, are you saying that we should TRASH Democracy, and Adopt a MONARCHY, or what? Indeed, I have always had it in my Warped Mind that "Capitalism is the Financial and Economic Salvation of Mankind!" So, is that not True, O Selected King? Must we Revert Back to the Dark Ages, when TYRANTS Ruled the World? †§‡

12-07 [_] Well, if you have not Noticed it, I would like to Remind you that Great Britain has the same Problem of having Extremely Rich and Extremely Poor People, who also Failed to Discover FREE Heating and Cooling, who Waste much Money, Time and Energy on it, which is also True of most of Socialist Europe, Communist Asia, Confounded Africa, and North America: beCAUSE of Vain and Silly TRADITIONS, and a Lack of Proper Tools to Work with; but, Certainly NOT for the Lack of hundreds of thousands of Mountains of ROCKS to Work with in this World of Wonders.

12-08 [_] So, O Elected King, have you ever Lived in a House that had Walls 10 feet THICK? And WHY should they be at least 10 feet thick?

12-09 [_] Well, I used to Live in a House that had Walls thicker than that, up to 17 feet thick, and it was quite Comfortable. However, the Roof was only 4 to 6 feet thick, whereby a certain Amount of Heat and Cold Penetrated it. Nevertheless, it Costed me nothing for Cooling, and only a small Amount of Wood for Heating. However, if I had it all to do over, I would not have Hesitated to make Stone Domes with 10 to 20 feet of Dirt and Rocks on Top of them and all around them: so as to take Advantage of the Good Earth, which Serves as a HEAT BANK and a COOLER, which Temperatures are Adjustable by Means of Windows / Skylights and Doors, which can be Opened or Closed as needed to Adjust the Inside Temperatures, which Requires Constant Attention; but, it is a lot Cheaper than Wasting 4 to 6 thousand Dollars per Year, just to Heat and/or Cool the House. Indeed, once the House is Finished, and the Inside Walls are 10 feet THICK, there is no Way that those Walls are easily going to Heat Up nor Cool Off. Therefore, if the Nights are Cool, the Doors and Windows can be Opened, in Order to Cool Off the House; and if the Days are Hot, the Doors and Windows can be Closed to Keep Out the Heat. However, if the Days and Nights are Extremely Hot during Hot Months of the Year, then the Doors and Windows must be kept Closed, except for a couple of Cracks, whereby a little Air can Circulate, without letting in a LOT of Heat, whereby Moisture will Automatically come into the House: beCause the Inside of the House is much Cooler than the Outside Temperature. Therefore, to Remedy that Humidity Problem, one must Build an Underground ICE HOUSE, which is much Cooler than the House, which has a Trap Door in the Floor of the House, or in the Ceiling of the Ice House, which is Opened to allow the Moisture to be Automatically Sucked Into the Ice House: beCause Moisture is always Attracted by Cold Things, including that Ice in the Ice House, which Ice can be Gathered during Freezing Weather, even as I have already Explained in other Books. {See www.Amazon.com for: **"The Right Design for Living!" (A List of Great Advantages for Building Beautiful Planned City States!) By The Worldwide People's Revolution!®** Book 012.}

12-10 [_] So, O Elected King of **"The New RIGHTEOUS One-World Government,"** it seems as though you have it all Figured Out, except for HOW to Persuade a Billion Young People to VOLUNTEER as Working Soldiers, whereby they might Build millions of Beautiful Planned City States, whereby almost everyone in the World can become Moderately Rich, huh? Indeed, they only Need to Humbly SUBMIT to your Master Plan, unless they can come up with a Better Master Plan, which I Seriously Doubt that they can Do: beCause your Master Plan comes from the Most High GOD, who Revealed to you **"Guaranteed Solutions!" (HOW to Solve our Local and Global Problems in the Most Rational Manner Possible!) By The Worldwide People's Revolution!®** Book 080. Yes, you are the only Person on the Whole Earth, who has those Guaranteed Solutions, which every Sane Person will Cheerfully Accept: beCause there are Zero Great Disadvantages for Building those **"GLORIOUS Swanky Hotels Castles and Fortresses!"**

(Beautiful Planned City States for WISE Intelligent Well-Educated People with Common Sense and Good Understanding!), Book 019! Therefore, **"All of the Arguments are in Favor of our Selected King, who has Zero Challengers!"** (Before you Attend another Election Deception, you should Carefully Study this Inspired Book with an Honest Open Mind!) By The Worldwide People's Revolution!® Book 085.

— Chapter 13 —

How to Persuade Millions of Young People to Join the Seven Great Swanky Armies of Voluntary Working Soldiers!

13-01 [_] One would not Think that it would be any Great Problem to Persuade any Young Unemployed Person to Join an Army of Voluntary Working Soldiers, seeing that all of them could make themselves Moderately Rich, just by their Labors, alone, while Earning 60$ per Hour for Installing Marble Tiles on the Solid Stone Walls of their own Houses and Home-craft Workshops. However, without GOOD Wages, you could hardly Persuade any of them to get Out of Bed, much less go to Work: beCause none of them are about to "Work for NOTHING." Indeed, being all-American-made, they would Naturally have no Faith in Working for **"Beautiful Swanky PALACES"** for everyone: beCause they Know for a Fact that they cannot Trust the Wicked Lying Federal Government, which has Lied to them hundreds of Times! Therefore, they would Naturally not Believe that any such Things could ever be Done, much less that they would Inherit Trillion-dollar Swanky Palaces, Tax-Free, Loan-Free, Interest-Free, and Insurance-Free! Yes, they would say, "I will have to See it Done, before I will Believe it, and even then I will Suspicion it to be another Capitalist Scam." Yes, they will say, "After we have Built all such Palaces, we will be Ordered to GET OUT: beCause we are not the Owners of them, in spite of doing all of the Hard Work. Therefore, what Guarantee is there that we will Inherit any such Palaces?" †§‡

13-02 [_] I would Think that any Young Unemployed Person would be most Happy to be Earning 60$ per Hour for Common Skilled Labor — such as Installing Marble Tiles on Walls, even if they did not get to Live within those Swanky Palaces. Indeed, I would be very Happy with those Good Wages, even if I never Inherited any Part of any Palace. However, I will Happily Sign my Name to the following Contract, which even a 12-year-old Boy can easily Understand:

A-[_] I, (Full Printed Name and Date of Birth of Potential Working Soldier — such as, April 21st, 1946 — The Innocent White Lamb from Angel Ridge, King's Mountain, Kentucky 40442)

, Agree to do an Average of 4 Hours of Common Skilled Labor per Day, or the Equivalent thereof — such as 8 Hours Today, and nothing Tomorrow; or, Work this Week, and have next Week Off — in Exchange for Living within a Swanky Palace, just as soon as we can get one or more Finished, which will Include my Clothing (Uniforms), Foods, Drinks, and whatever is Required for Living, without any Loans, Interest, nor Taxes: beCause I Understand that I am Exchanging that Time and Labor for my Living Expenses. Therefore, if I want to Earn some Money, I can go on Working for an Average of 8 Hours per Day, and be Paid According to **"A List of FAIR Swanky Wages!" (The Equitable Wage System!) By The Worldwide People's Revolution!®** Book 065. In other Words, if I do 4 Extra Hours of Work per Day, I can Earn as much as 400 Dollars per Day, and Save all of it: beCause all of my Expenses will be Covered by the first 4 Hours of Labor, including any and all Meals at any **Royal Swanky Buffet!** Moreover, I Understand that if I get Sick, or do not Feel like Working, I may Rest for as long as I Like at any **Swanky Fasting Sanitarium**, which will make it Possible for me to Totally Recover without Consuming any Drugs, Medicines, Pills, nor Poisons of any Kinds. I also Promise to Follow **"The Proper RULES for FASTING!" (The Complete Instruction Manual for True Repentance!)**, Book 046, whereby I will not Damage my Body in any Way, and might even become a HOLY Man. {See: **"HOW to Become a HOLY Man!" (40 Good Reasons WHY People Should FAST and PRAY!) By The Worldwide People's Revolution!®** Book 045.} Furthermore, when I am Working, I Promise to Do with all of my Might whatsoever my Hands Discover to Do, as if I were Doing it for GOD, and not for myself, nor for anyone else: beCause I Understand that it is GOD who Makes People Happy, and is the Great Judge of our Souls, and the Just Rewarder of both Good and Evil People. Therefore, if I do not Know HOW to Do something Correctly, I Promise to ASK FOR HELP, whereby I might Learn HOW, until I am Professional at the Skilled Labor that I Choose; or, at whatever Labor must be Performed for us to Prosper at the Time. Moreover, I Promise to not Sue anyone for any Reason: beCause I will be Free to Choose the People with whom I Want to Live and Work with, after Filling Out and Filing **"The Complete SURVEYS of our VALUES!" (SURVEYS of Religious Spiritual Political Governmental Sexual Social Moral Economic Business Labor Habitual and Miscellaneous VALUES!) By The Worldwide People's Revolution!®** Book 059. Yes, I Understand that I have to Fill Out and File those Surveys before I can Join any of the **"Seven Great Armies of Working Soldiers"**: beCause it is the only Rational Way for **"The New RIGHTEOUS One-World Government"** to Discover WHERE and with WHOM I Belong as a Member of that Good Government, whereby I can Live in Peace with other People of Like-mindedness, who can all Agree with this Contract, who Agree to Study: **"LIGHTNING STRIKES Versus Lightning Bugs!" (HOW you can Become Moderately RICH, without Telling any Lies nor Selling any Trash!) By The Worldwide People's Revolution!®**, Book 074, which Contains **"The New MAGNIFIED Version of the 20 Commandments,"** which I Promise to Learn, Believe, Love, and OBEY, whereby I will not have to Tax myself to Support any Police DEPARTments, Fire DEPARTments, Homeland Security DEPARTments, National Defense DEPARTments, nor any other Ridiculous DEPARTments! Indeed, it will Require a little Reading with a Capital R; but, I Seriously Doubt that it will make me Sick, Wounded, Crazy, nor Lazy. After all, I have never Discovered a more Ambitious Person on the Whole Earth than our Selected King, much less a Healthier nor Happier Person, who can Honestly say that he does not have a single Pain within his entire Body, who has Solid Evidences that he is an Honest Hardworking Person, who has never made a Slave of anyone, including myself, who would never Work for any TYRANT, nor Approve of the Greedy Selfish Heartless

Capitalist Economic System, which has Produced Billions of Unaware SLAVES, whom our Selected King has called Education Slaves, Work Slaves, Tax Slaves, Insurance Slaves, Interest / Usury Slaves, Rent Slaves, Credit Card Debt Slaves, Food Bills Slaves, Water Bills Slaves, Gas Bills Slaves, ElecTrickery Bills Slaves, Transportation Slaves, Repair Bills Slaves, Entertainment Bills Slaves, Telephone Bills Slaves, Internet Bills Slaves, Mortgage Bills Slaves, Childcare Bills Slaves, and Endless Bills SLAVES! Yes, I Believe in True Freedom with a Capital F, which will be the Case for me when I am Living within one of those **"Beautiful Swanky PALACES!" (A New Concept in Living Habits — Swanky Palaces for Poor People!) By The Worldwide People's Revolution!®** Book 066. Therefore, I shall be Wise for myself, and do my Best to make that Possible for as many Voluntary Working Soldiers as might Agree with me.

(Please Sign whatever Name that you might Like to Call yourself, since we have no Intentions of making any Investigations into your Background, and could care less if you are among the Worst of Violent Criminals: beCause we will get you Converted by one Means or another, beginning with Overwhelming LOVE! However, be Aware that you might be Banished from all Swanky Fortresses, if you Commit any Violent Crimes, and therefore you will Lose all of your Credit with us, and will have to Live with the Lions, Bears, Wolves, Coyotes, Foxes, Snakes, Skunks, Rats, Mice, Ticks, Fleas, Bedbugs, Lice, Chiggers, Mosquitoes, Fire Ants, and whatever might be Discovered in the Wilderness of Sins. Therefore, before you Lose your Temper, and Say and/or Do any Foolish Thing to some other Voluntary Working Soldier, just Remember that we have Counselors who can Help you to Solve your Problems, even if you must be Moved to some other Swanky Hotel, Castle or Fortress, whereby you can Live in Peace. After all, there will eventually be about 2 Million Swanky Fortresses! Therefore, just be Sure to Check the Correct Boxes in **"The Complete SURVEYS of our VALUES,"** whereby you will get Placed with Like-minded People. For Example, if you do not Like Thieves, just Check the Box: [_] I Promise to not Steal anything. [_] I Promise to not Murder anyone. [_] I Promise to not Marry anyone who does not Agree with my Beliefs, etc., etc.)

B-[_] I, (Please Print Full Name and Date of Birth of Potential Working Soldier),

Agree to Think and Act like a True Christian, according to Biblical Standards; and therefore, I do not have to Study any of the Inspired Books that are Listed in the A-Box above. In other Words, I am too Lazy to Study those Books; but, I Promise to be a Good Working Soldier, and Do whatever I am Asked to Do: beCause every Servant Needs a Good Master, and every Master Needs Good Obedient Servants, just to Prosper Correctly. {See: **"A Sound Argument for Masters and Servants!" (WHY Everyone Needs a Good Master, and every Master Needs Good Obedient Servants!) By The Worldwide People's Revolution!®** Book 008.}

(Please Sign your Full Legible Name and Present Date.)

C-[_] I, (Please Print your Full Name — Fictitious or not — and Date of Birth), Agree to be a Good Honest Muslim, Hindu, Buddhist, or whatever I am — God alone would Know for Sure: beCause I am Confused by the so-called "Christian" Doctrines, whereby I might Sin by Planting some Beans in a Garden. (See *Matthew 5—7, KJV.*)

D-[_] Do I have to Check one of the above Boxes with an X, just to get to Live within a Swanky Hotel?

E-[_] I am not Educated enough to be Qualified to Join any Swanky Army of Voluntary Working Soldiers. However, I Understand that even Grade School Dropouts are Welcome.

F-[_] I Fail to Understand why anyone on the Earth would NOT Want to Join one of the **"Seven Great Armies of Working Soldiers!" (HOW to Provide a Way for Everyone to WORK: so as to Eliminate Poverty, Crimes, Drug Abuses, Prisons and Unnecessary Taxes!) By The Worldwide People's Revolution!®**, Book 015, since they are all now Deprived of the 5,000+ Advantages for Living within them.

G-[_] God Knows that what the World most Desperately Needs is **"The New RIGHTEOUS One-World Government!" (HOW to Establish a Righteous One-World Government without Going to WAR!) By The Worldwide People's Revolution!®** Book 056. However, he is not Interested in FORCING People to Say nor Do what they do not Willingly Choose to Say nor Do. Therefore, People will just have to Suffer in their Miserable States of Extreme Poverty, until they come to their Riit Sensuz.

13-03 [_] I Reluctantly Checked the above Box in Verse 13-02: beCause it is too Good to be True. Besides that, such High Wages would Cause INFLATION, whereby it would Require no less than a Million Dollars to Buy a Plastic Bucket, which is made by a Machine, for a Cost of a couple Quarts of Oil. †§‡

13-04 [_] Well, in the Economic System that I Propose, there would be ZERO Inflation: beCause there would be ZERO Loans, and thus, ZERO Interest, which Causes Inflation: beCause there is no Money Printed to Cover the Cost of Interest Payments, whereby Money is Sucked Out of the General Supply of Money, even as Pastor Sheldon Emery explained in his Good Book, called: *Billions for the Bankers — and Debts for the People,* which you can Discover for Free on the Internet. Google it. Indeed, all of the Money would have to be EARNED by Honest Labor, whereby some Permanent Stonework Represents the Money that was Earned, whereby the Money has TRUE VALUE, even if it is only a Piece of Paper, which reads: **Wun Ower uv Komun Unskild Laaber**, which can be Traded for anything that is Worth one Hour of Common Unskilled Labor — such as a large Sweet Vine-ripened Organic Watermelon.

13-05 [_] So, if it only Requires a few Quarts of Oil to make that Plastic Bucket, then it will Cost the same as a few Quarts of Oil, or maybe 2$, since the Oil, itself, will be Free, like Water, Dirt, Sand, Gravel, and Rocks. Therefore, it all boils down to a Case of TRUST, huh? Indeed, if someone Trusts that Piece of Paper, and thus Accepts it as having the same Value as one Hour of Common Unskilled Labor, then it is Good Money, huh?

13-06 [_] Well, it is Equally as Good as any Money in the World, if People Trust it and Accept it as being Equally as Good as Silver and Gold, Diamonds and Rubies, or Marble and Granite. Indeed, the VALUE of the Paper is Depending on what it will "Buy," which, in this Case, is anything that is Worth one Hour of Common Unskilled Labor — such as Hoeing Weeds in a Garden. However, some Ambitious Young Man might Hoe 10 Times as many Weeds as some Lazy, slow-moving Sloth, whereby he is Worth 10 Times as much Money, Potatoes, Apples, etc.

13-07 [_] So, is there no Way to get Around the Money Game, just by everyone having his or her own Garden, Vineyard, Orchard, Home-craft Workshop, Sales Shop, and Beautiful Stone Dome Home Complex: beCAUSE of Establishing **"The New RIGHTEOUS One-World Government,"** which Drafts every Young Person in the World into those **Seven Great Armies of Working Soldiers**, in Order to Build Beautiful Planned City States for everyone in the World to Live within them, whereby each Family has its own Private Garden of Eden, you might say, whereby no one can be Unemployed from there onward: beCause of being Self-employed? Indeed, if someone Wants to Trade an Hour of Hoeing Weeds in a Garden for 10 Pounds of Cucumbers, he or she can Negotiate the Deal with whomever has Cucumbers and needs some Weeding done in the Garden. Otherwise, that Person can Grow his or her own Cucumbers in his or her own Garden, and also do his or her own Weeding, and Set whatever Value on his or her Work as he or she might Please. Moreover, he or she can put the Extra Cucumbers in Canning Jars, according to his or her Favorite Pickle Recipe. Otherwise, he or she can Sell or Trade his or her Cucumbers with whomever Wants them, and for whatever Free-Enterprise Price that they might Pay. †§‡ {See www.Amazon.com for: **"Seven Great Armies of Working Soldiers!" (HOW to Provide a Way for Everyone to WORK: so as to Eliminate Poverty, Crimes, Drug Abuses, Prisons and Unnecessary Taxes!) By The Worldwide People's Revolution!® Book 015.}**

13-08 [_] Well, I see no Good Reason to DRAFT every Young Person in the World, when almost all of them will Gladly VOLUNTEER, if they are Promised **Beautiful Swanky PALACES** to Live in, when they Complete only 6 Years of Common Skilled Labor, or the Equivalent thereof. After all, we can have and should have and will have Written Contracts to that Effect, whereby no one can be Cheated, and almost everyone will end up Living within a Beautiful Stone Dome Home Complex, whereby they will almost all become Moderately RICH! ‡

13-09 [_] I Checked the above Box 13-02 with an X, and Signed my Name below, after the A-[_], which is Equally as Good as any Legal Contract: beCause our Elected King is our Guarantee, if we can Discover one to Vote for. After all, our Selected King has already Died and gone to Heaven. Therefore, we will have to Discover another one, who is Equally as Good, or even Better. But, do not Ask me where to begin Looking: beCause I have no Idea. †§‡ {See: **"The Great Worldwide TELEVISED Court HEARING,"** Book 041, for the Answer.}

13-10 [_] Not everyone Wants to Live in a Swanky Palace. I Prefer a very simple Stone Dome Home with only 4 Rooms — such as a Living Room, Kitchen, Bathroom, and Bedroom. After all, I have a Good Capitalist Job, whereby my Standard of Living is already far above that of my Poor Deprived Naaberz. Therefore, I will just Continue to Drive my Gas-hog Car to Work, and Hope to God that Climate Changes do not Affect me. But, if Worse comes to WORSE, I can always Move myself to New Zealand, and take up Sheep Farming. †§‡§§

— Chapter 14 —

Working Soldiers Need Comfortable Living Spaces!

14-01 [_] I do not see any Need for Building small Cramped Apartment Houses, like the Russian and Chinese Communists did for their Peoples, when it is quite Possible and most Practical to Build LARGE Spacious Rooms for each Family, now that we are not Restricted by a Lack of Money, Building Materials, Working Soldiers, Proper Tools, Mechanical Slaves, and whatever we Need for TRUE Prosperity!

14-02 [_] What are we going to do — cover up the whole earth with ugly stone houses that have walls 10 feet thick?

14-03 [_] Well, since almost all of the Roofs will have Gardens on them, there will be no Lack of Space. Indeed, each Family Needs at least a one-acre Garden, which is about 200 feet by 200 feet, which Rests on the Roof of the Family who Lives below, INSIDE of the Terrace: so that each Person's Garden is directly in FRONT of his own House: so that he does not have to Climb up Stairs to get to his Garden. However, when he Wants to Visit his Naaberz in a Lower Terrace, or in a Higher Terrace, he simply walks to an Elevator or Stairway, whereby he can Visit them, even if he must get on a Subway Train with his Bicycle, Tricycle, Quadruped, Cart, or whatever: beCause the Trains will be large and spacious, having "Cars" that are 20 feet wide and 100 feet long, with Padded Leather-covered Seats all around the Inside Perimeters of them, if the Fortress is large enough to Accommodate all such Trains. Many People will Naturally Chose to Live in Small Planned Cities, which might not Need any Trains, at all, except to Connect with other Planned Cities by Underground Railways. I would Prefer to Live in a **FOURTH Swanky Lowtel Castle and Fortress**, which is Designed for Livestock and Gardens: so as to have LOTS of those LUSCIOUS All-Mineral Organic Gardens, Vineyards, and Orchards with Extra Sweet and Fragrant Fruits. Such Cities would be Surrounded by Hay and Grain Fields for the Livestock to Feed on, which would be Surrounded by Moats and Tall Stone Walls with Guard Houses and Bunkers for Protection. †§‡

14-04 [_] So, just how BIG would each Stone Dome be, if there is only one Acre to Build on?

14-05 [_] Well, if the Living Room Dome is 24 feet wide, having Joining Barrel-vault Tunnels to other Domes, which Tunnels are 10 feet long, that would be the Equivalent Space of 44 by 44 feet, which is 1,936 square feet; plus the Kitchen Dome, which is 20 by 20 feet, which would be 400 more square feet; plus 3 Bedroom Domes, which take up 16 by 16 feet of Space, times 3, equals 768 square feet; plus the Bathroom Domes, which would take up an almost equal amount of space: because of the Joining Barrel-vault Tunnels, or another 768 square feet; plus a Game Room, which is 20 feet by 20 feet, which is 400 square feet of space; plus the Workshop Dome, which is 30 feet by 30 feet, or 600 square feet of space; plus the Workshop Storage Dome, which is 400 square feet; plus the Sales Shop Dome, which is 24 by 24, or 576 square feet, which makes a Grand Total of 5,080 square feet of space. Therefore, having a Total of 44,100 square feet of space on one Acre

(210 feet by 210 feet), that would leave 39,020 square feet of space for anything else — such as Walk-in Coolers, Freezers, Bat Houses, Honeybee Houses, Offices, Storage Rooms, Cisterns, Ice Houses, Indoor Swimming Pools, Tunnels, Stairways, Elevators, and whatever — which seems like a Generous Amount of Space, to me. †‡

14-06 [_] So, if us Working Soldiers are Willing and Able to Do all of the Necessary WORK, is it Fair to say that we could have Living Room Domes that are 40 feet in diameter and 20 feet tall?

14-07 [_] Absolutely! You could have Living Room Domes that are 60 or even 100 feet in diameter; but, WHY? It just Means more Unnecessary CLEANING. Besides that, each Swanky Palace will have LARGE Comfortable Domes for Special Parties, Sports, Restaurants, Libraries, Game Rooms, Swimming Pools, Tennis Courts, Gymnasiums, Bowling Alleys, Pool Rooms, Churches, Mosques, Synagogues, Temples, Cathedrals, Concert Halls, Theaters, and whatever the Working Soldiers are Willing to Work for: beCause, from now on, no one will be Limited by a Lack of Money, nor by a Lack of Building Materials, Proper Tools, nor whatever is Needed for getting the Work Done by VOLUNTEERS, who must VOTE concerning all such Projects, and Check the Appropriate Boxes that they Agree with, whereby no one is made into a Slave. After all, if the Working Soldiers are Willing to Build Spacious Houses for themselves, why should they be Restricted by anything? Moreover, who cares whether or not it Requires 400 Years to get it all done, since someone will Naturally be Wanting to Earn more Money, which they might Want to Spend on Expensive Vacations? †§‡

14-08 [_] Will they not be Filling their Houses with Vain Things, which will eventually be Trashed in some Obnoxious Landfill? {See: **"The Environmentalists' Paradise!"** Book 035.}

14-09 [_] They will Produce High Quality Products for Sale, and no Junk at all. Therefore, the Trash Dumps will not be Filled with very much Trash, and certainly nothing like they are presently being Filled with. Most Containers will be Reusable, such as Glass Canning Jars, Fruit Juice Bottles, and other Containers. In other Words, we will have a much Better, Simplistic, Conservative Lifestyle, which will Require much less Energy. ‡

14-10 [_] I have always Wanted a 40-feet-long Hand-carved Cedar Clothes Closet, going all of the way around my 16-feet-wide Bedroom: so that I have a Different Suit to Wear each Day of the Year, along with 365 Pairs of Shoes to Cover Up my Ugly Feet. Moreover, I Want my own Home Theater for Watching the Movies, and Surround-sound Music in every Room of the House, including the Pool Room and Indoor Swimming Pool, which is Connected with other Swimming Pools by Means of Underground Tunnels: so that I can Fornicate, in Secret. †§‡§§

— Chapter 15 —

Working Soldiers are Contented to be Moderately Rich!

15-01 [_] I would be quite Happy to Live in a Modest Stone Dome Home Complex, whereby at least 4 Families could Live Well on just one Acre of Land (210 feet by 210 feet, or 64 meters by 64 meters): beCause there is no Way that a Family of 4 can Eat all of the Foods that can be Grown on one Acre. First of all, a single English Walnut Tree can produce a TON of Walnuts, which would Feed at least 20 Families all of the Walnuts that they might Want to Eat. Therefore, just one Tree per 10 Families should be Plenty. However, they Require a long Time to Grow, and can Live 200 Years, and take up a Space in a Garden that is 40 feet by 40 feet. Therefore, you could Grow only 25 such Trees on one Acre, or enough to Feed 250 Families one Pound, each Day of the Year, which is also True of Pecans, Hazelnuts, Almonds, and most all other Nut Trees: beCause, if they are Smaller Trees, they can be Grown in Smaller Spaces, and thus have more Trees. For Example, you can Plant Almond Trees every 20 feet apart, and have no less than 100 Trees on just one Acre, or about 1,000 Gallons of Almonds during a Good Year. Therefore, if you Ate nothing but Almonds, and a Quart of them every Day, it would Require no less than 4,000 Days to Eat them, or enough to Feed 16 People for 250 Days. However, no one is going to Eat that many Almonds, even if they are Tamari-roasted Almonds: beCause there are many other Fruits in the Gardens to Eat. In Fact, just one Cup of Almonds per Day would be Plenty of Food for most People, if they are not Working, who also Eat a Cup of Dates, some Lettuce, and a Pint of Carrot Juice, who might Live for 500 Years on such a Good Wholesome Natural Diet, if someone did not Break his or her Heart. †‡

15-02 [_] I Prefer to Eat a Great Variety of Foods, in Moderation, just to Enjoy the many Things that God has Provided for us to Eat; and therefore, 3 or 4 Walnut Trees within a Fortress of People like me, would be Plenty of Walnuts for 10,000 People. After all, if there were 6 or 7 Pecan Trees, 20 Almond Trees, 40 Hazelnuts, and 40 Pistachios, I would be Happy: beCause I Prefer Tacos, Burritos, Fajitas, Tostadas, Tortillas, Enchiladas, Entomatadas, Flautas, Spicy Frijoles, Molotes, Panuchos, Sopes, Guacamoles, Nachos, and Chilaquiles. (See *List of Mexican Dishes* in Wikipedia, which Links with a *List of Cuisines,* which are "Endless.")

15-03 [_] Well, not all Nut Trees Grow in the same Climate; and therefore, it would be Wise to Plant Extra Fruit and Nut Trees within each Fortress: so that all such Fruits and Nuts can be Traded with other Fortresses, whereby everyone will have a Greater Variety of Foods to Eat for their Sensual Pleasures. ‡

15-04 [_] You might Think that I am Crazy; but, According to my Way of Thinking, I could be quite Contented to Live in a Stone Dome Home that is only 40 feet in Diameter, which has Dividing Walls within the Dome for Various Small Rooms. For Example, the Kitchen could be 10 feet by 12 feet, and the Bedroom likewise, with a Bathroom 4 by 6.

15-05 [_] Well, if someone Agrees with you, they may Check that Box. However, where is your Home-craft Workshop in that Plan? Where is your Walk-in Cooler for the Produce that you Grow in your Garden? Where is your Pantry for a 7-year Supply of Canned Fruits and Vegetables, just in case there is a Great Famine: beCause of Climate Changes? Where is your Dining Room, just in Case you get some Visitors, and Want to Invite them to Eat with you? Where is your Game Room for the Children to Play in? {See www.Amazon.com for: **"HOW to Prepare for CLIMATE CHANGES!" (The Wisest Plan for Mankind to Follow!) By The Worldwide People's Revolution!® Book 004.**}

15-06 [_] I am a Bachelor, and have no Need for any of those Luxuries, much less a Large All-Mineral Organic Garden. {See the Link above or below for: **"The LUSCIOUS All-Mineral Organic Method of Gardening!" (HOW to Grow DELICIOUS Satisfying Foods for Potential Kingz and Kweenz in Swanky PALACES!) By The Worldwide People's Revolution!®**, Book 021, which is a Companion Book of: **"Orgimmick Gardening at its Best!"** Book 079.}

15-07 [_] So, without a Garden, what would you Do with your one-acre of Land?

15-08 [_] I would let it Grow up to Grasses for Feeding 2 Goats and a Sheep, which I would Sacrifice on the Altar in the Great World TEMPLE of PEACE! †§‡ {See www.Amazon.com for: **"The Great World TEMPLE of PEACE!" (The Glory of Jerusalem Arises Again!) By The Worldwide People's Revolution!® Book 017.**}

15-09 [_] Well, it makes no Difference to me what you do, just as long as you Live with other People of Like-mindedness, even if all of you are Crazy. After all, you could have many Fruit and Nut Trees, while also having those 2 Goats and a Sheep on the same Ground, just as long as the Trees are Protected from those Beasts, who might Kill them. The Sheep would be less Harmful. The Goats would likely Eat the Leaves, Eat the Fruits, Eat the Bark, and KILL the very Tree that is Feeding them: beCause they are Typical Capitalists, of the Republican Religious Sect, who are Unaware of what is Happening in the World, who even Deny that the Past 10 Years were the Hottest in History, and 2014 holds the World's Record Number of Hot Days — Thanks to Capitalist Hogs, who are too Lazy to Plant some Fruit and Nut Trees, and Attend to them, Properly, whereby the Earth might be more Shaded, as Opposed to Covering Up the World with Hot Asphalt Pavements in Parking Lots, Shopping Mauls, Highways, Driveways, Streets, and Hot Tarred Roofs. Yes, it is now Time to Cooperate with the Good EARTH, and Live like Sane People on the Land that Feeds and Clothes us. †§‡ {See the above link for: **"Poverty Hunger Riots Strikes Brutalities Election Deceptions and Civil Wars!" (The High Price that we Earthlings have Paid for Leaving the Good Land!) By The Worldwide People's Revolution!® Book 014.**}

15-10 [_] I Prefer to Continue to Live just Exactly the Way that I have been Living, even if it Destroys the Whole Earth. After all, we only Live ONCE. †§‡ (See *Hebrews 9:27.*)

— Chapter 16 —

Working Soldiers should be Spiritually-minded!

16-01 [_] I could care less about any Stone Dome Home Complex, Garden, Vineyard, Orchard, Cisterns, Home-craft Workshop, Sales Shop, nor even a Self-air-conditioned Tornado-proof House, just as long as I have someone to Love. After all, I can always Work in a Fish Canning Factory, if I need more Money. Otherwise, I Prefer to Live on a Boat in the Ocean, whereby I can Meditate on the Goodness of God, and Dream about going to Heaven when I Die. †§‡§§

16-02 [_] Well, "to each his own," as they say. You are Welcome to Say and Do whatever makes you Happy, just as long as it is not Violent nor Destructive. After all, we all have our Freedom; but, not with a Capital F: beCause, even if we are Free to Breathe Fresh Clean Air, it does not Mean that we can Obtain it. Likewise, even if we are Free to Eat Good Wholesome Natural Foods, it does not Mean that we can Obtain those Foods. Moreover, even if we are Free to Live in Fireproof, Hail-proof, Termite-proof, Mouse-proof, Rot-proof, Paint-proof, Tornado-proof, Insurance-proof, Self-air-conditioned Stone Dome Homes with Polished Marble Walls, it does not Mean that we can Afford them: beCause of the Great False Economy. Furthermore, even if we are Free to Live in Peaceful Cities without any Criminals, it does not Mean that one such City Exists on the entire Earth. Therefore, of what Value is our so-called "Freedom," if we cannot Use it? ‡

16-03 [_] The Most Important Thing in Life is to have a Personal Relationship with Jesus Christ, which we can Obtain by Celebrating Christmas, whereby we Honor his Birth; and then we should Celebrate the Death and Resurrection of Jesus during Easter Holy Days, whereby he Blesses us for Sincerely Believing that there are 3 Nights and 3 Days from Friday Night until Easter Sunrise on Sunday, just as it is Written in *Matthew 12:40.* †§‡§§

16-04 [_] Well, if you can Count 3 Nights and 3 Days from Friday Night to Sunday Morning, you should go back to Grade School, and Learn HOW to Count. Moreover, while you are Counting, how about Counting how many TRILLIONS of Dollars have been Wasted on Christmas Trash, Easter Nonsense, 4th of July Celebrations, Halloween Trash, Thanksgiving Dinners, and Unhappy New Year's Celebrations, which never Profited anyone anything! Yes, how about Adding Up the High Costs of Perfumes, Paints, Make-up, Toilet Tissues, House Cleansers, Shoe Polish, and all of the Vain Things that People can Live HAPPILY without! †‡

16-05 [_] If God did not Want us to have all of those Toys, Drugs, and Vain Things, why did he Inspire People to Invent them? {See www.Amazon.com for: **"Did God or Satan Ordain Medical Doctors??" (Ask Huck Finn and/or Nigger Jim: because neither Tom Sawyer nor Judge Thatcher would Know!) By The Worldwide People's Revolution!® Book 022.}**

16-06 [_] The Devil Inspired Foolish People and Greedy People to Invent them, and only Ignorant Fools would Buy them, when there are much Greater Priorities in Life. For Example, how Long could People Survive without Water? Therefore, everyone Needs a Good 7-year-long Water

Supply. † {See: **"HOW to Get our PRIORITIES in ORDER!" (The Glories of Democracy; and, Does DEMON-ocracy have its Priorities in Order?) By The Worldwide People's Revolution!®** Book 060.}

16-07 [_] I will take my Chances on the Rain, which is quite Reliable, even in Californicate. †§‡

16-08 [_] You speak as one of the Foolish Women have spoken, who put a Higher Priority on a New Car, than on a Large Cistern for Water Storage, in spite of going to the Local Church of Graceful Sinners, who are about as Spiritually-minded as Toads and Croaking Frogs.

16-09 [_] And just how would you know how Spiritually-minded those Toads and Frogs are?

16-10 [_] Well, having no Words to Communicate with, it is Doubtful that Toads nor Frogs have ever Considered any Spiritual Subjects to Think about — that is, IF they can Think, at all? I have my Doubts that they can: beCause of a Lack of Words to Think with. Moreover, you can See similar Blank Faces in American Classrooms, where Children are Daydreaming about anything except the Subjects at hand: beCause those Schools are quite Boring. However, when they find themselves in the middle of a Great Famine, with nothing Good to Eat, perhaps they will Reconsider the Goodness of my Inspired Books, and even Remember that I Offered to make almost all of them Moderately Rich, if they would simply Elect me to be their Righteous King. However, being Deceived Americans, they just Naturally Reject the Notion of having a King of any Kind, without Realizing how Unprepared they are for a Big Disaster, such as a 3.5-year-long DROUGHT, whereby a third of Mankind will DIE from the Great Famine! — and all for the Lack of those **"GLORIOUS Swanky Hotels Castles and Fortresses!" (Beautiful Planned City States for WISE Intelligent Well-Educated People with Common Sense and Good Understanding!) By The Worldwide People's Revolution!®** Book 019. Yes, it will be a little too Late when the Rain STOPS; and it WILL Stop, according to *Revelation 11,* unless the Masses of People REPENT, which they are not very likely to Do: beCause that Implies that they will have to STOP EATING and DRINKING, and head up to Mount Sinai with Moses, or head to Mount Horeb with Elijah. {See www.Amazon.com for: **"The Gospel According to our Elected King!" (The Good News from the Most Modern Perspective!),** Book 013, plus: **"God Speaks and the Whole World Listens!" (Fire on the Mountain from the Burning Bush by the Spirit of Truth!),** Book 026, plus: **"The PRAYERS of PUMPKINHEADS!" (Even God Needs a Little Humor to Cheer himself Up!),** Book 007, plus: **"The Proper RULES for FASTING!" (The Complete Instruction Manual for True Repentance!) By The Worldwide People's Revolution!®** Book 046.}

— Chapter 17 —

Potential Working Soldiers will DEMAND "The Great Worldwide TELEVISED Court HEARING!"

17-01 [_] If you do not Understand what **"The Great Worldwide TELEVISED Court HEARING"** is all about, it is only beCause you have not Studied: **"LIGHTNING STRIKES Versus Lightning Bugs!" (HOW you can Become Moderately RICH, without Telling any Lies nor Selling any Trash!) By The Worldwide People's Revolution!®**, Book 074, which goes into all of the fine Details. However, just to Sum it all up in a Condensed Form, I will now give to you a Synopsis or Summary of it.

17-02 [_] First of all, we must Understand that most People in the World Know for a Fact that we have BAD Leaders and very BAD Governments, or else the World would not presently be in such a Sorry Condition. Secondly, we must Understand that all of those Wicked Leaders should be brought to TRIALS, whereby they can be found Guilty of their High Crimes in Low Places, and thus be Deposed, or gotten Rid of, which is what **"The Great Worldwide TELEVISED Court HEARING"** is all about, which must be Televised to all People in all Nations, and in all Major Languages, who must Act as the GRAND JURY, who must Listen Carefully to all of the Evidence, and then Decide what to Believe, and whom to Trust. After all, they have never been Given that Opportunity: beCause the Whole Truth about almost all Subjects has been Repressed and Suppressed, whereby the Masses of People have no Idea that it is Possible and most Practical for all of them to become Moderately RICH! Indeed, many of them still Sincerely Believe that Riches are only Good for Rich People, and that Poor People do not Deserve any such Riches: beCause, "they have not EARNED those Riches by going to Universities, whereby they might have gotten their Proper Credentials, Diplomas, Awards, Certificates, and thus 'Authority,' whereby they might be Worthy of such Riches," as one very Bright Student Observed, who had no Desire to Waste 4 more Years in the Universal College of almost Worthless Knowledge, just to be "Qualified." After all, just how much "education" does one Need for Flipping Hamburgers in some Greasy "Fast Food" Joint, where 80 to 90 percent of College Graduates begin their "Careers": beCause those "High-paying Jobs" were not Available when they Graduated? ‡ {See www.Amazon.com for: **"Are you a Jobless Graduate of the SKQL uv FQLZ?" (HOW to get a GOUD EJUKAASHUN without Robbing the Bank!) By The Worldwide People's Revolution!®** Book 020.}

17-03 [_] So, are you saying, O Selected King, that it is Possible for a Grade School DROP OUT to Mix Up Mortar, and Set Marble Tiles on a Concrete Wall, without having a College Education, nor even a Degree in Mental Rapeology? †§‡

17-04 [_] Well, that is certainly one Good Way to state that Fact of Life, since almost any 12-year-old Boy could Learn HOW to Mix Up Mortar and Set Tiles on a Wall, even if he could not "Reed" nor "Riit": beCause it is a SKILL, which can only be Learned by DOING IT, or at least by Watching it being Done, whereby the Procedure can be Copied, which is True of almost all Manual

Labor Professions. However, there is much more to Living Skills than merely Setting Tiles on a Wall, and Planting Trees in a Garden; but, one is not apt to Learn those Living Skills by Attending some Universal College of almost Worthless "knowledge," which does not even Capitalize Faith, Hope, Trust, Love, Patience, Persistence, nor Obedience — which are **"The Seven Basic Spiritual Building Blocks of LIFE"** — beCause of not Realizing the Importance of all such Good Things! Yes, without those Good Attributes, a Person is apt to Remain in the Darkness of Ignorance, FOREVER! Moreover, almost none of those Attributes are Taught in the Public School of Ignorant FOOLS! {See www.Amazon.com for: **"The Public School of IGNERUNT FQLZ!" (HOW we have been GRAATLEE DISEEVD by Capitalism!)**, Book 024, plus: **"In thu Beeginingz uv Thingz!" (Thu Kreeaashun Stooree frum thu Beegining!) By The Worldwide People's Revolution!®** Book 025.}

17-05 [_] So, O Selected King, is it Fair to say that ALL Governments should be TRASHED?

17-06 [_] Well, if they do not Agree to Establish **"The New RIGHTEOUS One-World Government"** and thus make it Possible for almost all People to become Moderately Rich, just by their Labors, alone, then I would say that they should all be TRASHED: beCause they are Obviously Working for the Synagogue of Satan, whereby Rich Edomite Bankers, Rich Edomite Insurance Agencies, Rich Edomite Drug Companies, Rich Edomite News Networks, Rich Edomite Book Publishers, Rich Edomite Weapons Manufacturers, Rich Edomite Oil Industries, and other Rich Zionist Edomites are only getting Richer and RICHER, while the Masses of People are getting Poorer and POORER — Thanks to a Zionist Edomite Economic System called CAPITALISM, which Utilizes the Edomite Stock Market to Promote Edomite Products, whose Chief Edomite Business is Selling DRUGS. However, some People might Argue with that, and Claim that the Chief Edomite Business is LOANING MONEY for the Purpose of Collecting USURY or INTEREST, whereby Edomite Bankers have raked in no less than a hundred TRILLION Dollars! Meanwhile, hundreds of millions of People do not even have Running Water in their Houses! Moreover, Billions of People barely Survive from Paycheck to Paycheck, and have a Stack of Bills to be Paid: beCause they have Fallen into Edomite TRAPS, which can all be Proven in a Courtroom with Law and Order. Yes, it MUST be Proven at **"The Great Worldwide TELEVISED Court HEARING,"** so that almost everyone in the World can Learn about the EVILS of the Capitalist Empire, which must be put Out of Business, if Humanity is to Survive: beCause Capitalism is Responsible for most of the Evils in the World: beCause it is the *"Love of Money"* in Action, on Steroids, you might say, whereby a few People have made themselves Extremely Monetarily Rich, while the Vast Majority of the People are Suffering in their States of EXTREME Poverty, when it was Possible and most Practical for almost all People to become Moderately Rich, in all Ways, and Live like Kings and Queens in **"Beautiful Swanky PALACES!"** †‡

17-07 [_] So, are you saying, O Selected King, that Rich People do not LOVE US? How else would we have "American Castles," if it were not for Rich People, like William Randolph Hearst and George Washington Vanderbilt? (See *Wikipedia* on the Internet for the Evidence.)

17-08 [_] Well, it is True that they Love your Money, and will Say and Do just about anything to get as much of it as Possible: beCause their entire Evil Empire is Established in such a Way as to make Work Slaves, Tax Slaves, Interest Slaves, Drug Slaves, Insurance Slaves, Sex Slaves,

Childcare Slaves, Drunkards, Gluttons, and Diseased Idiots of almost all Peoples, who have Accepted it as the "best way to live," but, NOT Capitalized, as in: "The Best Way to LIVE," whereby they might all become Moderately RICH, and never get Sick nor Diseased, and thus never Need the "Services" of Medical Snakes! {See www.Amazon.com for: **"Did God or Satan Ordain Medical Doctors??" (Ask Huck Finn and/or Nigger Jim: because neither Tom Sawyer nor Judge Thatcher would Know!)**, Book 022, plus: **"HOW to Become a HOLY Man!" (40 Good Reasons WHY People Should FAST and PRAY!) By The Worldwide People's Revolution!®** Book 045.}

17-09 [_] So, it Sounds to me like we have been Lied to, O Elected King, and not just one Time; but, all of the Time, ever since we were Born! Yes, those Rich Edomites have been Advertising and Selling Packs of Lies to us for well over a hundred Years! Indeed, it began with the Sales of Cigars, Cigarettes, Coffee, Cokes, Cocaine, Cooked Concoctions, Candies, Cookies, Cakes, Iced-Creams, Cheeses, Cheese Cakes, and other Confections and Conceptions, whereby most of us have become Addicted to all such Evil Things, while Imagining that those are GOOD Things! However, it can be Proven in a Courtroom that all of those Things are BAD for our Health, and should be Illegal to Sell them: beCause they are ADDICTIVE! However, People must be Given FREEDOM to Choose HOW they Want to Live, and with WHOM they Want to Live: so that they can make Fools or Saints of themselves. My Guess is that most People would Choose to Live with the Saints, if they were Given the Opportunity to Do so: beCause, who is it that does not Love Good Honest Trustworthy Hardworking Righteous People — such as Jesus, Peter, Paul, and Mary? Yes, we all LOVE them: beCause they are Most Lovable, who were Contented with Natural Wholesome Foods and Drinks, who had Good Health, and such Perfect Health that they could Heal other People, just by their Shadows! ‡ (See *Acts 5:12—16, KJV.*)

17-10 [_] Well, there is only One Way that those Saints will be Reproduced, and that is IF we, the Masses of People, DEMAND **"The Great Worldwide TELEVISED Court HEARING,"** whereby we might all Learn the WHOLE Truth about ALL Important Subjects, including the Subjects of Good Health and True Prosperity, which does not Include any of the Pollution in this World of Woes, much less ALL of the Pollution of Air, Water, Land, Oceans, Lungs, and Bodies! Indeed, there is a Way to Prosper without hardly any Pollution, and Certainly without the Use of any Drugs, which all of the Children should Learn about: so as to not become Future Tax Slaves, Insurance Slaves, Drug Slaves, Interest Slaves, Work Slaves, and Capitalist Prostitutes! Therefore, we, the People, must make a BIG ISSUE about it, and Relentlessly Pursue JUSTICE for ALL! {See the above Link for: **"Poverty Hunger Riots Strikes Brutalities Election Deceptions and Civil Wars!" (The High Price that we Earthlings have Paid for Leaving the Good Land!) By The Worldwide People's Revolution!®** Book 014.}

— Chapter 18 —

Good Working Soldiers are not Afraid of the Whole Truth!

18-01 [_] You might not be Old Enough to Remember the Radio Broadcasts during the 1950's and 60's, when Cigarettes were Advertised between almost every Popular Song that was Played on the Radio, and the next Song: beCause it was Legal to have all such Advertisements, even though it was also known at that Time that Smoking Caused Cancers. Indeed, it was a very Lucrative Business for the Synagogue of Satan, who are still Selling all such Addictive Things: beCause they are PROFITABLE. Yes, Gaining more MONEY is the Principle Objective of the Capitalist Economic System, which is Anti-Christ: beCause Christ's Main Objective or Goal would be for everyone to have GOOD HEALTH, even though the *"Holy" Bible* does not make that Subject Crystal Clear by any Means. However, the *King James Version* is so Bold as to Quote Jesus, saying:

> The thief cometh not, but for to steal, and to kill, and to destroy: I am come that they might have life, and that they might have *it* more abundantly. — John 10:10.

18-02 [_] So, if you look up the word, "life" in Strong's Exhaustive Concordance, in the Greek Dictionary, you Discover that "Life" actually Means "Good Health," huh? Therefore, Jesus was saying:

> The Thieves and Medical Snakes come not, except for to Steal and Rob you, and even Kill and Murder you: because they Seek to Destroy you, after getting as much of your Money as Possible; but, I am come so that my Sheeps might have Good Health, and so that they might have it more Abundantly.

18-03 [_] Well, that is Technically more Accurate, and also in Line with the Realities of Life, which is an Obvious Thing: beCause, if Medical Doctors and the Federal Government were Seeking our Good Health, WHY would the single most Addictive Drug still be Legally for Sale? Well, I will tell you why — it is beCAUSE it is very Profitable for Edomite Drug Pushers, who could care less whether or not you Die with Cancers: beCause they are also Collecting Trillions of Dollars for "Cancer Research," in spite of Knowing for a Fact that it is our Unnatural Lifestyles that are Causing those Cancers. Yes, they even Confess that our Bad Air is Responsible for many Lung Diseases; and God alone would know just how many Diseases are Caused by Bad Water, Bad Foods, Bad Living Habits, and so on. However, rather than DEMAND that all such Issues should be Proven in a Courtroom, whereby the Chief Criminals might be Found GUILTY, and thus Sentenced to Prisons with Satan, the Devil, those Medical Doctors just Smile and Carry on! Likewise, the Politicians just Smile and Carry on: beCause no one can Fight Against the Biblical BEAST, and Win! (See *Revelation 13:4.*) Yes, WHO can make War Against America, the Mother / Producer of Prostitutes and Abominations? Trust me, that Mysterious "Beast" that arose out of the Sea is the United States of America, whose Deadly Wound was Healed after the Revolutionary

War, and the Unholy Stock Market was Established, whereby almost all Nations *"Wandered after the Beast,"* just as it is Written, who also Set Up their own Stock Exchanges, even as far away as China, which is on the other Side of the World. Yes, they too have Fallen into the Capitalist Pit that was Dug for them by Americans, who are Working for the Dragon, for the Synagogue of Satan, the Devil, just as *the Book of Revelation* Reveals in its Mysterious Way, which is Highly Camouflaged, even as my own Inspired Books are Highly Camouflaged: beCause it is Necessary to HIDE the Whole Truth, whereby those Lying Zionist Edomites cannot Discover it, until it is too Late for them to Destroy it: beCause of being Spread all about by Zealous Truth Lovers, who say to their Ignorant Naaberz: "Guess what? — there is a Way to put all of those Wicked Politicians OUT of Business, just by DEMANDING what our Selected King calls: '**The Great Worldwide TELEVISED Court HEARING!**' Yes, he Proposes that we Work Slaves, Tax Slaves, Interest Slaves, Insurance Slaves, Drug Slaves, Sex Slaves, and Endless Bills Slaves GO TO BED, and Stay in Bed, and Refuse to get Out of Bed: beCAUSE of becoming SICK of those Lying Edomites, until those Wicked Politicians DEMAND 'The Great Worldwide TELEVISED Court HEARING,' whereby we Tax Slaves might Learn the WHOLE Truth about all Important Subjects, and thus VOTE for whatever we Believe to be the Best Way to Live, AFTER we have Learned ALL of the Evidences! Yes, we Tax Slaves must become SICK of those Sorry Politicians, and so Sick that we simply go to BED, come next April 21st — rather than Protest or Riot in the Streets: beCause their 'Achilles Heel' is MONEY and the Great False Economy, which is Based on a Foundation of LIES and Deceptions, which cannot Resist **'The Swanky Sword of Divine Truths,'** which can Cut Off the Head of Lies with one Swift Stroke!" And their Ignorant Naaberz will say something like this: "What do you Mean? I have no Idea what you are Talking about." And those Wise People will say, "Do you not Understand that we Tax Slaves have been Voting for 2 or 3 WRong Political Parties for Centuries, and nothing is getting any Better? In Fact, everything is only getting Worse and WORSE! Indeed, Statistics show that we Americans are now 147 Trillion Dollars in Debt to those Greedy Edomite Bankers, who were never Needed: beCause a Righteous GovernMINT simply Mints and Prints the Necessary New Money — NOT to Give it Away to Ignorant Fools; but, in Order to Use that New Money WISELY, in Order to HIRE whomever is Willing and Able to Learn and Work, in Order to Help Build Beautiful Planned City States, whereby we can Solve all of our Massive Problems, including those Hateful Wars, while making ourselves Moderately RICH, just by our Labors, alone, without any Loans, without any Interest, without any Taxes, and without any Insurance: beCause those **GLORIOUS Swanky Hotels Castles and Fortresses** are Fireproof, Mouse-proof, Termite-proof, Rot-proof, Paint-proof, Hail-proof, Tornado-proof, Hurricane-proof, Self-air-conditioned, Tax-proof, Insurance-proof and Usury-proof: beCause God's Selected King will simply HIRE US to Build them — that is, if we are WISE, and thus Elect HIM to be our Righteous KING!" And those Ignorant Naaberz will say something like this: "Those Lying Zionist Edomite Bankers will never Forgive us of the Great Debts that we Owe to them." And those Wise People will Answer them, "When we Establish **'The New RIGHTEOUS One-World Government,'** those Friendly Banksters will just FORGIVE US for all of our Debts: so that we can Celebrate the Great Year of JUBILEE and Walk Out FREE and HAPEE!" And those Ignorant Naaberz will say something like this: "And WHY would they Want to Forgive us of a 147 Trillion-dollar Debt, when all such Money must be Paid Back to them: beCause the Full Faith and Credit of the United States Government Depends on it. Indeed, if we do not Pay Off our Debts, those Friendly Banksters will not Loan any more Money to us, whereby we might Build our little Stinking Plastic Outhouses and Cockroach Dens, which are the Envy of all of the People in the World, who Want similar Firetrap Mouse-infested Cockroach Dens to Live in, whereby they can also Pay 5 to 6 thousand dollars per Year for Heating and Cooling Bills, plus Property Taxes: so that all of the little Children can get a 'Good Education' with a Capital E, whereby they can become Future Tax Slaves, Insurance Slaves, Interest Slaves, Drug Slaves, Sex Slaves, and Work Slaves, whereby they can be Depressed and Oppressed, more and more, until at Last they are Ready to RIOT in the Streets, and BURN DOWN all of those Wooden / Plastic Firetrap Houses, just so that those Friendly Bankers can be Properly Repaid! After all, they were the Unholy Ones who Loaned the Money for Building them: beCause they Judged that all such Houses are GOOD; or else, they would not have Loaned any Money for Building them! Is that not Correct?" And those Wise People will say, "Well, you may now Test them, and thus Discover what Spirit they are of, just by Asking them if they will Loan any Money to you to Build your own Little PANTHEON, like the one in Rome, which has Stone Walls 17 feet THICK, which has no Heating nor Cooling Bills, no Fire Insurance, nor any Need for such Vain Things, whereby you will Discover the Truth of it — that those Friendly Banksters will not Loan to you a single Dime to Do that: beCause they LOVE those Edomite Insurance Companies, Edomite Chemical Corporations, Edomite Plastic Manufacturers, Edomite Better Homes and Gardens Magazines, Edomite Cook Books, Edomite Drugs, Edomite Hospitals, Edomite Research Laboratories, Edomite Chemistry Labs, the Edomite DEPARTment of GOOD Drugs and BAD Foods Administration, the Edomite DEPARTment of Agricultural Deceptions, the Edomite DEPARTment of Poor Housing and Bad Urban Renewal of TRASH DUMPS, the Edomite DEPARTment of National Insecurity Agencies, the Edomite DEPARTment of Homeland Insecurity, the Edomite DEPARTment of Financial Deceptions Administration, the Edomite DEPARTment of Injustices, the Edomite DEPARTment of National Defenseless Insanity, and the Edomite DEPARTment of Election Deceptions!" And those Poor Ignorant Naaberz will Respond with something like this: "I never knew that we had so many Edomite DEPARTments in this Country of Con Artists, whereby we now have no less than 20 Million BureauRATS, including the Federal Burden of Investigation (FBI), and the Central Unintelligent Agencies (CIA), of which there are no less than 30 Top Secret Agencies without any Public Names at all; plus the Bureau of Alcoholics Tobacco and Firearms Fanatics (BATF), the Federal Emergency Mismanagement Agency (FEMA), and the U.S. Immigration and Customs Enforcement (ICE), which is as Cold-blooded and Coldhearted as a SNAKE, which has Deported Millions of Immigrants, who only Wanted to Raise their Standard of Living, by WORKING, which is something that ICE would know nothing about: beCause of being Frozen Solid, whereby Parents can be taken away from their Children, Legally, and Deported! Yes, oh such HAPPY Children, whose Minds have been Wounded and Damaged for Life, who are still Stuttering." And those Wise People will say, "It is now Time to bring all of those High-ranking Criminals to COURT, and not Allow them to get by with any more Major Crimes." And those Poor Enlightened Naaberz will say, "We have always Believed that this is the Greatest Nation in the World; but, now we are Learning that it is all a Charade and a FARCE: beCause, if the Federal Government Truly Loved us, they too would DEMAND **'The Great Worldwide TELEVISED Court HEARING,'** whereby we might all Learn the WHOLE Truth about a RIGHTEOUS One-World GovernMINT, which has an Abundance of Money for HIRING all of us Seven Great Swanky Armies of Voluntary Working Soldiers to Build those Beautiful Planned City States, which are Designed for LIVING and PROSPERING, at HOME, without any Loans, without any Interest, without any Taxes, without any Insurance, and without any Bills to Pay for anything: beCause of being set FREE by the Inspired Words of Provable Truths! Yes, Jesus said, *'You shall Learn the Truth, and the Whole Truth will Set you Free when you Practice it.'* — *NMV of John 8:32.* Therefore, it is just a Matter of Learning those Provable Truths, and Publishing them to ALL Peoples, Worldwide: so that they can Decide whether or not they Want to be Future Tax Slaves, or Free People with a Capital F!" And those Wise People will say, "Well, if you Presently Love all of these Provable Truths, will you Help our Selected King to Sell his Good Books, whereby everyone in the World might Learn about the Fall of Babylon, which Means CONFUSION? Yes, will you Help to bring the Evil Empire to an END?" {See www.Amazon.com for: **"The Low Court of Supreme Injustices is Brought to Trial!" (Our Elected King Butts Heads with the United States Supreme Court, with or without their Black Robes of Hypocrisies and Lies!)**, Book 011, plus: **"The Right Design for Living!" (A List of Great Advantages for Building Beautiful Planned City States!)**, Book 012, plus: **"The CONSTITUTION for the New RIGHTEOUS One-World GovernMINT!" (How all Peoples can get True Justice, and Celebrate the Great Year of JUBILEE!)**, Book 016, plus: **"The Great World TEMPLE of PEACE!" (The Glory of Jerusalem Arises Again!)**, Book 017, plus: **"GLORIOUS Swanky Hotels Castles and Fortresses!" (Beautiful Planned City States for WISE Intelligent Well-Educated People with Common Sense and Good Understanding!)**, Book 019, plus: **"The BIG White OUTHOUSE on the Not-so-Biblical Capitol DUNGHILL!" (The Chief Sins of the Divided States of United Lies!) By The Worldwide People's Revolution!®** Book 023.}

18-04 [_] I Checked the above Box for Verse 18-03: beCause I Agree with all of the Provable Truths within it. However, it does seem to be a very Long Paragraph.

18-05 [_] Well, if you Imagine that it is a very Long Paragraph, you should read: **"For the Love of Money!" (The Strange Things that People Say and Do to Get more Money!)**, Book 003, which contains a certain Chapter, called: **Nigger Jim Explains what a True Nigger IS!**, which is no less than 8 Pages Long! Yes, it is just one Long Sentence, if you can Believe it, which Means that if it is brought up in a Courtroom, the entire Sentence must be Read Aloud from the Beginning to the End, just to have all of the Words in Context: so that nothing is taken Out of Context, which is WHY the Low Court of Supreme Injustices is not very Interested in bringing our Selected King to Court: beCause it would Require no less than a hundred Years to Try him for that one Paragraph: beCause of having to Read it again, each Time that a certain Phrase is Questioned, just to make Sure that it is not taken Out of Context with the Remainder of the Words, whereby the Jury might have it Perfectly Clear within their own Minds, whereby they might not Misjudge any Subject! ‡

18-06 [_] I must Confess that you are a rather Tricky Fellow, O Selected King; but, what will you do when the Low Court of Supreme Injustices brings you to Trial for Disturbing the PEACE in this Country, after all of those Cities of Confusion have been BURNED to the Ground: beCause of your Hateful Suggestive Literature? Indeed, the above Verse 18-03 is Suggesting that we Light those Ugly Plastic Houses on FIRE, unless those Banksters Agree to FORGIVE US of all of our DEBTS! After all, who can more easily Afford to Forgive us, seeing that they are all RICH, and have far too much Money, while we Tax Slaves, Insurance Slaves, Interest Slaves, Drug Slaves, Sex Slaves, Childcare Slaves and Work Slaves have NONE!?

18-07 [_] Well, Verse 18-03 might SEEM to be Suggesting such an Evil Thing; but, I FORBID IT to be Done: beCause it would Cause a LOT of Needless Sufferings. Indeed, it would be a Million Times Better for those Wicked Politicians to DEMAND **"The Great Worldwide TELEVISED Court HEARING,"** and thus Avoid any such Calamities: beCause it is Possible and most Practical for the Great False Economy to Continue, just as it is, until we get almost all of those **GLORIOUS Swanky Hotels Castles and Fortresses** Finished, and the Furniture Moved into them; and then it will not Matter whether or not all of those Cities of Confusion are TRASHED: beCause we can Live quite Happily without them and those Lying Zionist Edomite Bankers, Edomite Medical Doctors, Edomite Drugs, Edomite Research Laboratories, Edomite Chemical Corporations, Edomite Paint Factories, Edomite Weapons Manufacturers, Edomite Book Publishers, Edomite Movie Makers, Edomite Cosmetics Manufacturers, Edomite Diamond Cartels, Edomite Drug Cartels, Edomite Psychiatrists, Edomite Holocaust Hoaxers, and so on! Yes, the Prophecies in *the Book of Revelation* will all be Fulfilled, and no one will Buy their Merchandise anymore, and the Tax Slaves will go Free! Yes, the Prisons and Jails will all be Opened Up for whomever Repents, and they will also Walk Out Free! ‡

18-08 [_] O Selected King, I can hardly Believe it! Are you saying that even Bernie Madoff can Repent and thus go Free? How about OJ Simpson, James Holmes, and Dylann Storm Roof?

18-09 [_] Well, if they Truly Repent, we can Forgive them, including those Lying Edomites, who should be getting their Confessions Prepared, Accurately, right now: beCause it will Cut Down of the Costs of that Great Meeting of the Most Intelligent Minds, called: **"The Great Worldwide TELEVISED Court HEARING,"** which you can read all about in Book 041, which everyone in the World should Study: beCause it is Full of Truths and Wisdom.

18-10 [_] Okay, O Selected King, I will Submit to **"The Swanky Sword of Divine Truths,"** and Study it. However, if I Discover something that Disagrees with my Religious and/or Political Upbringing, I will Reject the entire Book, and not Recommend it to anyone else.

— Chapter 19 —

Good Working Soldiers will not Reject the Entire Mountain of Truths for any Minor Faults!

19-01 [_] O Selected King of **The Worldwide People's Revolution!®**, I must Confess that I just LOVE your Long Paragraphs — such as Verse 18-03, which really Turns On my own Inspiration, and more than you might Imagine. For Example, I have Met many People who have been Highly Offended by something that I have Said to them about some Phony Religious Beliefs of theirs, which I did not Deliberately say to Offend them; but, that is HOW they Accepted it, as if I were Trying to put them Down, when I was only Trying to Correct them. However, it is Obvious that I was not very Diplomatic, you might say, or else I would have Won their Hearts by Word-craft. After all, if a Man can Manage his Words Correctly, he might even be Able to Persuade the most Stubborn Enemy to Agree with him; but, it Requires TIME to Do all such Things. Yes, it Requires much PATIENCE, which few People have, nowadays: beCause everyone seems to be in a Big Hurry, as if going to their own Funerals, you might say, who can hardly Wait to get there! Yes, it is another Paradox of the Human Mind, which even William Shakingspears would no doubt find it Difficult to Explain: beCause it is such a Strange Paradox.

19-02 [_] For Example, I once Met an Old Lady, who Weighed no less than 450 Pounds (or about 204 Kilograms), who Suffered with a whole List of Ailments, many of which I never Heard of before she Informed me, with whom I Attempted to Explain a few Important Things about Good Health, and how to Obtain it for FREE. Indeed, you must Understand that she was Spending well over a thousand Dollars per Month on MediSINZ, and God knows what else; and therefore, I Tried to have Compassion on her, and Explain a few Important Things to her; but, she Claimed to not have Time to Hear me out: beCause she "had things to do." Well, she nearly drove away in her Car, which was Resting itself under a Shade Tree with her Inside of it, and me Standing Up on the Outside of it, by her front Window, which was rolled down. So, I said to her, "Hold on a minute, my Wife has been Baking Cookies this Morning, and I can Smell them. Would you not like to have some?" And she said, "O yes, that would be nice." So, I went into the House and told my Wife that she would like some Cookies, which she Delivered in Person to the Big Fat Lady in the Car, who had much in Common, who got into some Normal Conversation about their Ailments, which went on for no less than 2 Hours, and maybe 3 or 4: beCause I went to do other Things after 2 Hours, rather than Stand there for the Remainder of the Day, Listening to her Ailments, you might say. Well, at any rate, I brought a Chair for my Wife to Sit herself on, so that she could Rest, since all of the Cookies were Finished Baking; and thus the 2 of them Shared their Cookies and Ailments, you might say, and Naturally came up with the same Conclusion as they did during Times Past — that none of those Medicines were Repairing their Ailments; but, that by Chance or otherwise, some Doctor Snake might Discover some Shot of Puss or Magic Pill that might Cure them, if not Kill them with some New and Strange Form of Cancer: beCause of Mixing Up the New Drugs with the Old Drugs. After all, there were Warning Labels on most of the Bottles of MediSINZ that they were Consuming, whereby whole Lists of Bad Side Effects were Presented for anyone who might Fear to Use them with Alcohol, which seemed to be the Worst of Bad

Combinations. Perhaps the Liver cannot Handle so many Toxic Poisons at the same Time; but, for some Reason, Totally Beyond me to Figure Out, neither my Wife nor her Extra Heavy Friend could Understand that perhaps the Drugs, themselves, were making them TOXIC. Indeed, I Tried to Explain it to them; but, they were Sure that neither the Doctor Pill Popper, nor the Doctor Puss Shooter would be Prescribing any Medicines that might Damage them too much. After all, they had College Degrees, being "educated" People, you might say, being more Intelligent and perhaps Wiser than Almighty God, whose Trillions of Wild Animals have never Suffered with any such Ailments, nor ever Consumed even ONE of those Pills nor Shots of Puss. Well, at any rate, it was Futile to even Try to Communicate any such Truths to such Sick-minded People: beCause they had Obviously been "Sold Down the River into Drug Slavery with Nigger Jim," as Mark Twain might say, who could not be Expected to Know much of anything about any Subject, much less something about Latin MediSINZ with Long Unreadable Names, which not even Medical Doctors can Pronounce Correctly, which they often shorten up by Abbreviating them. †§‡

19-03 [_] For Example, DDT is actually DII-kloor-oo-DII-fu-niil-TRIK-kloor-oo-eth-aan, which is hardly pronounceable, unless it is written in "Funetik Ingglish," which has one Way to Spell one Sound, every Time, even if you are Drunk on Drugs. You may look up DDT in any Dictionary, and thus Discover that I am not Lying to you. Indeed, *Wikipedia* has whole Lists of Chemical Abominations for you to Study, if you are Interested in any such Things. I much Prefer to not Torment my Mind with them. Nevertheless, my Wife and her Fat Friend carried on for Hours and Hours, talking about their Ailments, while those so-called "Important Things" that she had to Attend to somehow got Forgotten about: beCause they Obviously were not nearly so Important as getting some much-needed Attention from my Wife, who also Needed some Attention in a Courtroom, whereby she might have herself Straightened Out to some Degree: beCause she Insists on Eating, when she should be Fasting. However, she does not Sit all Alone in the Courtroom of Public Opinions. No sir, she has the Company of no less than 100 Million Americans, who also find it Extremely Difficult to STOP Eating! After all, they are only Bombarded with a Minimum of 1,204 Advertisements per Day on TV, which are Suggesting that they should EAT; and behold, they DO Eat: beCause they are now "Programmed" to Eat and EAT, whereby only a Slight Suggestion is enough to Trigger them to get into the Chips and Dips DEPARTment of the Gross Grocery Stores: beCause they are Naturally HUNGRY! In Fact, they are Literally STARVING to Death while EATING and FEASTING! Yes, that is the Truth of it: beCause they are Deprived of Wholesome Natural Foods, which might Satisfy them. †§‡ {See www.Amazon.com for: **"The LUSCIOUS All-Mineral Organic Method of Gardening!" (HOW to Grow DELICIOUS Satisfying Foods for Potential Kingz and Kweenz in Swanky PALACES!) By The Worldwide People's Revolution!®**, Book 021, plus: **"Did God or Satan Ordain Medical Doctors?" (Ask Huck Finn and/or Nigger Jim: beCause neither Tom Sawyer nor Judge Thatcher would Know!) By The Worldwide People's Revolution!®** Book 022.}

19-04 [_] So, have you been Growing those Good Fruits and Vegetables for your own Wife to Eat?

19-05 [_] Well, I Tried it; but, she did not like them; and therefore, I gave it up. After all, there is nothing very Sensual about Eating Sweet Corn from the Organic Garden, even if that Corn Tastes ten times Better than normal corn from a Gross Grocery Store: beCause a Good Cook can always Spice that Corn with some Maaunaaz, Cheez and Chilee Peperz, whereby it will Actually Taste Better to them than Good Natural Wholesome Sweet Corn from the Garden, which is Best if it is

Eaten RAW, and Immediately: beCause it has more Vitamins in it, if it is FRESH. In other Words, remove the Corn from the Stalk, shuck it clean, and stand right there in the Garden to EAT IT! Yes, if it is Truly GOOD Corn, it will not Require any Additives, Preservatives, nor even Salt: beCause it is Naturally Sweet and GOOD, being Immature, Tender, and just Riit. However, it Requires far too much Effort to Produce all such Sweet Corn. Besides that, if you do get it Growing in the Garden, some Sneaky Raccoon will Discover that Patch of Corn, and thus Invite all of his or her Friends and Relatives to Descend upon those Stalks of Corn during the Darkness of Night, and thus go from Stalk to Stalk, just to TASTE of them; and behold, if they do not Taste just Right, they will go to the next Stalk, and Break it Over, and Taste of that Corn — until, within an Hour or less, the entire Patch of Corn will be RUINED! Yes, I Remember when we first Moved to the little Farm, I was passing by a Naaber'z Garden, when he was in Church, if you can Believe it; and there were no less than 100 of those Raccoons in his Garden, at about 11 A.M., who Scampered Away into the Woods when they Spotted me Walking by. Therefore, I went over there to that Corn Patch to Inspect it; and behold, not one Cob of Corn was left Standing on a Stalk in its Natural Condition: beCause those little Thieves had come to Destroy that Garden; and thus I said to myself, "He needed a good wall around this garden." However, I did not have those words Capitalized within my own Mind, as I should have: beCause he Needed a GOOD Stone Wall around his Garden with a Moat around it, with a Slick Polished Granite Wall, whereby no Raccoon with Wet Feets could have Crawled Up such a Wall, much less have Passed Over an Overhanging Roof on the Wall, which has a Slick Underbelly, you might say, which is Designed to Cause those Raccoons and all other Creatures to SLIP OFF and into the Moat, which has a Crocodile or 2 in it! †§‡

19-06 [_] So, what did that Gardener Think about the Condition of his Corn Patch, after getting Home from Church Services?

19-07 [_] Well, I Swear to God that he Baptized that whole Garden with a Flood of Curse Words that would have Em-bare-assed the Devil, himself! Yes, it was near unto Hellfire and Brimstone coming Out of his Foul Mouth. Therefore, I said to him: "Did they Teach to you all such Things in Church this Morning?" And he said, "Hell NO — I Learned those Things from my Daddy, who had the same Problem with those Damned Raccoons!" And I said, "Well, what you Desperately Need is a LOT of Money, whereby you might Build a Proper Stone Wall around that Garden." And he said, "But, there is no Banker in the World who would Loan Enough Money to me for Building such a Proper Stone Wall: beCause they would all Argue that it only Needs an Electric Fence around the Garden; but, I cannot even Afford to do that: beCause God has not Blest me with Enough Money." And I said, "Are you Sure that God has something to do with it, or is it the Fault of the False Government, which should have an Endless Supply of New Money for doing Good Works?" And he said, "What are you saying?" And I said, "Did they not Teach to you anything about Money in the School of Fools?" And he said, "Why are you Speaking Evil of our Good Government and their Public Schools? I think that you should go to Church, and Learn to have Respect for the American Flag: because this is the Greatest Nation on the Earth." And I said, "If that is True, why are you so Poor?" And he said, "Well, I have to make Interest Payments to the Bank for the Money that I Borrowed for Buying this little Farm and that Tractor over yonder." And I said, "I Prefer to Live in the Woods, and go Hunting for a Raccoon to Eat, whereby I am Free from all such Debts." And he said, "Yes, but you do not have a Wife and a half dozen Children to Feed." And I said, "That is not True: because I do have a Wife, which you can read about in *the Book of Revelation,* which is called *the Bride of Christ,* who has not made herself Ready for the Second Coming of the Anointed Savior, who will not Return for an Unholy Bride." And he said, "What do you Mean?"

19-08 [_] And I said, "Well, do they not Teach to you anything in that Backward Church of Graceful Sinners? Do they not Know the *Scriptures* at all? Are they Unaware that the Bride of Christ must be HOLY, which would be the Opposite of some Tub of Lard that is Filled with Cancers?" And that was all that he could Tolerate from my Undiplomatic Mouth, whereupon he scooped up an Ax, and was about to Throw it at me, when I ran away: beCause his Wife was also another Big Tub of LARD, you might say, who was much more Religious than he was, who had "red" the *"Holy" Bible* from Cover to Cover no less than 20 Times, and still did not Discover *Revelation 22:11.*

19-09 [_] There is not one Cockroach in the City Dump who could Understand *Revelation 22:11.*

19-10 [_] That is beCause it is a Mutilated Book. Indeed, it reads as if to say, *"If you are Holy, you shall still be Holy during the Judgment Day; but, if you are Unholy, you shall still be Unholy during the Judgment Day. Moreover, if you are Filthy, and Die in your State of Filthiness, you shall still be Filthy during the Judgment Day."* However, that is NOT what it is Stating, is it?

— Chapter 20 —

The Conclusion

20-01 [_] It is a Wonder that such a Person did not get Murdered for using such Offensive Phrases as a "Tub of LARD that is Full of Cancers." Does the *Bible* Teach People to be so RUDE? †§‡

20-02 [_] Well, it does Refer to Fat Walruses in *Psalm 78:31,* which is probably Offensive to all such People: beCause it Causes them to Feel Guilty: beCause of a Lack of Self-Discipline, which is Understandable. However, when we Hold **"The Great Worldwide TELEVISED Court HEARING,"** it will be very Easy to Correct all such People: beCause only one Good Example is Needed for Correction, and she can be as Fat as a Hog when we Lock her up in a Fasting Sanitarium, if she Volunteers for it; and when she comes Out, she will be as Slender and Happy as a New Baby, Guaranteed! Therefore, all such Fat People can Stop Murdering themselves at their own Tables, and in their own Couches, by Eating and EATING; and take up: **"The Gospel According to our Elected King!" (The Good News from the Most Modern Perspective!) By The Worldwide People's Revolution!®** Book 077. Yes, they can now Escape from the Prison of Lies through the Doorway of Confession, if they will. Otherwise, they will be Cursed with the Seven Last Great Plagues, and be Branded with the Mark of the Beast! Guaranteed! †§‡

20-03 [_] I much Prefer to Join one of those **Seven Great Swanky Armies of Voluntary Working Soldiers**, whereby I will not have to Suffer through any Great Famine, nor be Cursed with any Plagues, nor be Branded with any Mark of the BEAST.

20-04 [_] Well, you are a Wiser Person than most People, who are really SLOW to Catch on to what is Happening. Indeed, my Guess is that they will put Off the Day of their Salvation, until it is Everlastingly too Late to Save themselves from the Great Famine that is Coming, when it Stops Raining for 3 Years and 6 Months. (See *Revelation 11.*)

20-05 [_] It seems as though you Rely a whole lot on that *Book of Revelation,* O Selected King; and I find that rather Disturbing: beCause it is an Unreliable book, which Contradicts other Books in the *Bible,* which are probably also Unreliable, being Inventions of Lying Edomites. †§‡

20-06 [_] Well, say whatever you like about the *Bible,* and even Mock it, if you please; but, you cannot Rightly Deny that the *Holy Bible* does Contain many Provable Truths, which just have to be Sorted Out from among all of the Lies, some of which are Far Beyond Belief, if you Think about them — such as that Noah's Ark Story, and the Golden Statue of King Nebuchadnezzar, which was Supposedly 193 feet Tall, 42 feet Thick, and 60 feet Wide, being made of SOLID GOLD, which King Neb Supposedly Erected in the Plain of Dura, which no one has ever Found, and which no Ancient Books even Mention: beCause it was just another Bad Dream that King Neb had, which got Mistranslated, which is WHY it is Best to Study the New MAGNIFIED Version, which makes all such Things Crystal Clear. †§‡

20-07 [_] And what makes you Imagine that we can TRUST the New MAGNIFIED Version, since it is NOT a Translation of any Biblical Words from any Book?

20-08 [_] Well, can you not Trust the Spirit of Truth? Can you not Sense when you are Reading TRUTHS, O Croaking Frog? Trust me, the Truth will not Kill you to Study it; but, it is Possible that Lies and Liars will Destroy you and the entire Nation. ‡

20-09 [_] I should Think that the Rejection of Truths is the Greatest of all Sins: beCause it Causes all of the other Sins. Therefore, it is not Wise to Reject any Provable Truth, even if it is about what Actually Happened during September 11th, 2001. (See www.AE911TRUTH.org for the Evidence, as well as whatever Dr. Judy Wood might have to say about it, who is no Liar.)

20-10 [_] Well, it is for Sure that all such Issues can be Settled at: **The GREAT Worldwide TELEVISED Court HEARING!**" Yes, whatever the Controversy might be, it can only Rightly be Settled in a COURTROOM! Therefore, let us Work Slaves, Tax Slaves, Interest Slaves, Insurance Slaves, Drug Slaves, Sex Slaves, and Endless Bills Slaves DEMAND that Great Meeting of the Most Intelligent and Well-Educated Minds, before we Blast ourselves to Hell with Atomic and Hydrogen BOMBS! After all, it might be a little Em-bare-assing for certain so-called "Leaders," who have been Hiding the Truth from us; but, for most People, it will be a Great Day of REST and RELIEF from the Stresses of Living; and especially when we Celebrate the Great Wedding of the Most Humble Honest Nations in Jerusalem, in the Great World TEMPLE of PEACE! Therefore, whatever you Do, do NOT Allow anyone to make you into another Murderous Soldier: beCause GOOD Soldiers do not have to be MURDERERS! NOTE: For your Enlightenment and Entertainment, see www.Amazon.com for the following Inspired Books.

— Chapter 21 —

A Long List of other Fascinating Literature by the same Inspired Author

[_] 21-01 — **"LIGHTNING Versus the Lightning Bug!" (HOW almost Everyone can become Moderately RICH, without Telling Any Lies nor Selling Any Trash!)** Book 001.

[_] 21-02 — **"What is WRong with those Professing Christians?" (A Self-Examination of the Heart of the Body of Good Government!)** Book 002.

[_] 21-03 — **"For the Love of Money!" (The Strange Things that People Say and Do to Get more Money!)** Book 003.

[_] 21-04 — **"HOW to Prepare for CLIMATE CHANGES!" (The Wisest Plan for Mankind to Follow!)** Book 004.

[_] 21-05 — **"Why do I have to be Surrounded by CRAZY PEOPLE!" (Do almost all People Feel like they are Surrounded by CRAZY People??)** Book 005.

[_] 21-06 — **"The Washington Journal is a FARCE! (C-SPAN Managers are not very WISE!)** Book 006. (This Book has lots of Good Humor.)

[_] 21-07 — **"The PRAYERS of PUMPKINHEADS!" (Even God Needs a Little Humor to Cheer himself Up!)** Book 007. (Some of it is for Adults only.)

[_] 21-08 — **"A Sound Argument for Masters and Servants!" (WHY Everyone Needs a Good Master, and every Master Needs Good Obedient Servants!)** Book 008.

[_] 21-09 — **"WHY are some Preachers so POOR?" (HOW almost all Preachers could Get Moderately RICH, without Preaching any Outlandish LIES!)** Book 009.

[_] 21-10 — **"GOOD NEWS for REBEL WOMEN!" (HOW almost all Wives can become Moderately RICH without Leaving their Homes! Guaranteed!)** Book 010.

[_] 21-11 — **"The Low Court of Supreme Injustices is Brought to Trial!" (The Worldwide People's Revolution!® Butts Heads with the United States Supreme Court, with or without their Black Robes of Hypocrisies and Lies!)** Book 011. (This Inspired Book contains the Famous *Declaration of Interdependence,* which is a Must Read. It also contains the Correct Wording for the Placard on the Statue of Liberty.)

[_] 21-12 — **"The Right Design for Living!" (A List of Great Advantages for Building Beautiful Planned City States!)** Book 012. (This Book contains many Important Drawings, as well as HOW to Save hundreds of Trillions of Dollars by Building Swanky Fortresses, and Living in Peace within them. It is a Companion Book of Book 011, which contains many more Great Advantages for Fortresses.)

[_] 21-13 — **"The Gospel According to The Worldwide People's Revolution!®" (The Good News from the Most Modern Perspective!)** Book 013. (This Book contains the Famous Sermon of Jonah to the Ninevites, whereby 120,000 People Repented in Sackcloth and Ashes! Do not Miss Out on it.)

[_] 21-14 — **"Poverty Hunger Riots Strikes Brutalities Election Deceptions and Civil Wars!" (The High Price that we Earthlings have Paid for Leaving the Good Land!)** Book 014.

[_] 21-15 — **"Seven Great Armies of Working Soldiers!" (HOW to Provide a Way for Everyone to WORK: so as to Eliminate Poverty, Crimes, Drug Abuses, Prisons and Unnecessary Taxes!)** Book 015. (This Book contains a True Life Story when I was in the Army.)

[_] 21-16 — **"The CONSTITUTION for the New RIGHTEOUS One-World GovernMint!" (HOW all Peoples can get True Justice, and Celebrate the Great Year of JUBILEE!)** Book 016.

[_] 21-17 — **"The Great World TEMPLE of PEACE!" (The Glory of Jerusalem Arises Again!) By The Worldwide People's Revolution!®** Book 017.

[_] 21-18 — **"The Swanky Associations of Working Soldiers!" (A Fascinating Collection of Various Kinds of Voluntary Working Soldiers!)** Book 018. (There will be thousands of Associations for all Kinds of Occupations, which will Specialize in Fine Arts — such as Hand-carved Leather-bound Books. See **"LIGHTNING STRIKES Versus Lightning Bugs!"** Book 074, for a Good Example.)

[_] 21-19 — **"GLORIOUS Swanky Hotels Castles and Fortresses!" (Beautiful Planned City States for WISE Intelligent Well-Educated People with Common Sense and Good Understanding!)** Book 019. (This Book contains many Rough Drawings, which could be Greatly Improved upon by someone who Knows the Art, and has the Correct Computer Programs for doing it.)

[_] 21-20 — **"Are you a Jobless Graduate of the SKQL uv FQLZ?" (HOW to Get a GOUD EJUKAASHUN without Robbing the Bank!)** Book 020. (This Inspired Book contains the New MAGNIFIED Version {NMV} of *First Corinthians 13,* plus: HOW to Produce Pure Living Water!)

[_] 21-21 — **"The LUSCIOUS All-Mineral Organic Method of Gardening!" (HOW to Grow DELICIOUS Satisfying Foods for Potential Kingz and Kweenz in Beautiful Swanky PALACES!)** Book 021. (This Book Explains HOW to make a Flood-proof Garden, while Trapping the Rainwater.)

[_] 21-22 — **"Did God or Satan Ordain Medical Doctors?" (Ask Huck Finn and/or Nigger Jim: because neither Tom Sawyer nor Judge Thatcher would Know!)** Book 022. (This

Inspired Book Reveals HOW to Prevent Common Colds, and has a Special Chapter that Explains what a True "Nigger" IS. Surprise yourself!)

[_] 21-23 — **"The BIG White OUTHOUSE on the Not-so-Biblical Capitol DUNGHILL!" (The Chief Sins of the Divided States of United Lies!) By The Worldwide People's Revolution!® Book 023.** (This Book contains Special Words that most People have never Heard! Surprise yourself again!)

[_] 21-24 — **"The Public School of IGNERUNT FQLZ!" (HOW we have been GRAATLEE DISEEVD by Capitalism!)** Book 024. (This Book Teaches Children HOW to "Reed and Riit in Funetik Ingglish in just wun Daa!" You should Challenge your Frendz and Naaberz with it.)

[_] 21-25 — **"In thu Beeginingz uv Thingz!" (Thu Kreeaashun Stooree frum thu Beegining!)** Book 025. {The Cover Photo shows a Picture of a Golden Supootaa (Sapote), which not one Person in a Million has ever Tasted: because it does not Ship very well, in spite of it being one of the most Sweetest Pleasant Fruits known to Mankind, which must Ripen on the Tree to be Extremely Good, after it is Grown Properly by **"The LUSCIOUS All-Mineral Organic Method of Gardening!"** Book 021, which Means that the Topsoil must have all of the Proper Minerals in it. Remember the Grapes of Eschol, which the Children of Israel brought back from the Promised Land in the *Book of Joshua,* which Required 2 Strong Men to Carry just one Cluster! See the Fascinating Photos in: **"Orgimmick Gardening at its Best!" (HOW to Grow Delicious Satisfying Foods without a 10-Million-Dollar Investment!) By The Worldwide People's Revolution!® Book 079.}**

[_] 21-26 — **"God Speaks and the Whole World Listens!" (Fire on the Mountain from the Burning Bush by the Spirit of Truths!)** Book 026. (This Powerful Book contains the Best Noah Story of all of the Books, including that of Gilgamesh the Great of Ancient Babylon!)

[_] 21-27 — **"Does a Good Soldier have to be a MURDERER?" (Seven Great Swanky Armies of Voluntary Working Soldiers!) By The Worldwide People's Revolution!® Book 027.** (Chapter 03 contains a True Life Story about a Dog Pile, which happened to me when I was just 10 Years Old.)

[_] 21-28 — **"Thu Nq MAGNUFIID Verzhun uv Thu PROVERBZ uv KING SOLUMUN in Plaan Ingglish!" (The Understandable Version of the Famous Proverbs of King Solomon in Plain English!)** Book 028. (This Marvelous Book MAGNIFIES each Proverb unto the Glory of the Great God of Inspiration, which is taken from the Original 4,000-page Book, which was written in less than 2 Months by the GIFT of Inspiration, which also contains the Famous Proverbs of Queen Izubelu!)

[_] 21-29 — **"UNLIMITED ENERJEE 99 Percent Pollutions Free!" (HOW to Obtain FREE ElecTrickery, Worldwide!) By The Worldwide People's Revolution!® Book 029.** (This Book contains the Jackson Brower Suicide, among many other Fascinating Subjects.)

[_] 21-30 — **"FREEDUM uv SPEECH!" (U Speshoul Maguzeen uv Onist Upinyunz!)** Book 030-0001, which contains the Great Advantages for Using Swanky Mulching Rocks in an All-Mineral Organic Garden, plus Baptism by Fire and Speaking in Foreign Languages! It is a Must

Read. The Cover Photo shows a Portion of the Author's Marbleous Indian Countertop or Food Bar, which is just one Example of what you can also have in your own **"Beautiful Swanky PALACES!"** if you have the Honesty, Faith, Hope, Trust, Love, Patience, Persistence, Cooperation and OBEDIENCE that are Required for True Prosperity! Therefore, Ejukaat yourself, and you will be Glad that you did!

[_] 21-31 — **"A Sure Cure for GUN VIOLENCE!" (HOW TO STOP GANG WARS and CRIMINAL SHOOTINGS!) By The Worldwide People's Revolution!®** Book 031. {The Cover Photo shows a Picture of a Short Shotgun, which is Fully Loaded with Double 00 Shells, and is Ready for any Tax Master who might Attempt to Steal the Retirement Home, who never moved a Finger to Help Build the Rock Houses, whereby we moved more than 66,666,666 Pounds by Hand, whose Property was Cunningly Stolen by that False Anti-Christ WICKED Cover-up Government, which allowed Bankers to Rob us of 30 Years of Hard Labor and more than 300,000 dollars-worth of Investments in our Uncommon American Farm, which is Explained in: **"LIGHTNING STRIKES Versus Lightning Bugs!" (HOW you can Become Moderately RICH, without Telling any Lies nor Selling any Trash!) By The Worldwide People's Revolution!®** Book 074, which contains many Photographs with Profound Explanations! Do not be left out in the Darkness of Ignorance. Get Informed, now: beCause, **"The Great False Economy is now DEBUNKED!"** Book 053.}

[_] 21-32 — **"AIIRMWVC and Reasonable Solutions!" (Aliens, Illegal Immigrants, Refugees, Migrant Workers and other Victims of Capitalism!) By The Worldwide People's Revolution!®** Book 032. (This Inspired Book contains *the New MAGNIFIED Version of Job 33.*)

[_] 21-33 — **"Mark Twain Races for the PRESIDENCY!" (The 2020 Presidential Candidates Desperately Need Some STRONG Undefeatable COMPETITION!) By The Worldwide People's Revolution!®** Book 033. {This Book contains a Part of my Autobiography, and my Personal Answers to the Questions in **"The Complete SURVEYS of our VALUES!" (SURVEYS of Religious Spiritual Political Governmental Sexual Social Moral Economic Business Labor Habitual and Miscellaneous VALUES!)** Book 059. It also contains many Black and White Photographs.}

[_] 21-34 — **"ECCLESIASTES UNCOVERED!" (The New MAGNIFIED Version of Ecclesiastes and the Song of Solomon in Plain English!)** Book 034. (This is the Book that contains the Famous Sayings for *"There is a Time to be Born, and a Time to Die ..."* which has been Greatly Magnified!)

[_] 21-35 — **"The Environmentalists' Paradise!" (HOW almost Everyone could be Living in a Beautiful Manmade Paradise!) By The Worldwide People's Revolution!®** Book 035. (This Book contains the NMV of *Psalm 48,* which will Amaze you, O Lady Doubtfulness!)

[_] 21-36 — **"The Seven Basic Spiritual Building Blocks of LIFE!" (Faith Hope Trust Love Patience Persistence and Obedience!)** Book 036. (This Book contains the Mockingbird's Version of *Hebrews 11,* plus the NMV of *First Corinthians 13,* among many other "Goodies.")

[_] 21-37 — **"DIETS!" (A Reasonable Solution for the "Eternal Controversy"!) By The Worldwide People's Revolution!®** Book 037.

[_] 21-38 — **"The Nature of CAPITALISM!" (A List of the EVILS of CAPITALISM!)** Book 038.

[_] 21-39 — **"SWANGKEENOMIKS Rules the Roost!" (HOW all People can Prosper in a RIIT WAA, and STOP Polluting the Earth with Capitalist TRASH!) By The Worldwide People's Revolution!®** Book 039. (The Cover Photo shows a Portion of our Retirement Home, before the 5,000+ square-feet Concrete Roof was Installed, after moving more than 66 Million Pounds by Hand!)

[_] 21-40 — **"The New MAGNIFIED Version of The Book of MOORMUN!" (The Story of the White and Dark Indians in the Americas!)** Book 040, which comes in 2 Volumes of about 500 Pages, each. The Cover Photo on the First Volume shows the Queen of England's Golden Coach, and the Cover Photo on the Second Volume shows one of many Polished Spanish Marble Walls in our Retirement Home, which is worth a thousand dollars per square yard, which is another Example of what you can also have, if you simply OBEY your Righteous KING! All such Marble is very Inspiring. No one could Study it for very long without Believing in a Great Creator God. The Picture does not do it Justice. You would have to See it in Person, and Wash it with Pure Water to bring Out the Beauty.

[_] 21-41 — **"The GREAT Worldwide TELEVISED Court HEARING!" (That Great Meeting of the Most Intelligent and Wel-Ejukaatid Miindz!) By The Worldwide People's Revolution!®** Book 041. {This is the Book that the World has long been Waiting for: beCause it will Overthrow the Evil Empires, and make it Possible to Establish **"The New RIGHTEOUS One-World Government!" (HOW to Establish a Righteous One-World Government without Going to WAR!) By The Worldwide People's Revolution!®** Book 056. This is the Greatest Idea since the Invention of the Light Bulb, Guaranteed!}

[_] 21-42 — **"The Secret City of the Great King!" (HOW the True Church will Escape from the Great Tribulation!) By The Worldwide People's Revolution!®** Book 042. (Be Sure to Inform your Friends, Relatives and Naaberz about this Wonderful Book: beCause they might also Want to Escape!)

[_] 21-43 — **"Terrorists Beware that your Days are Numbered!" (HOW to Bring those Terrorist Attacks to a Screeching HALT!) By The Worldwide People's Revolution!®** Book 043. (This Book also contains the Fascinating Book of LEHI, which has now been Restored!) †‡

[_] 21-44 — **"The New MAGNIFIED Version of ISAIAH in Plain English!" (The Understandable Version of the Book of Isaiah!)** Book 044. (The Cover Photo shows a Swanky Potato and Avocado Salad with Sweet Peas and Corn, among other "Secret" Ingredients, which are Revealed within the Book. Remember that you can read many Words for Free in the Book Previews on Amazon.com.usa.)

[_] 21-45 — **"HOW to Become a HOLY Man!" (40 Good Reasons WHY People Should FAST and PRAY!)** Book 045, which is a Companion Book of:

[_] 21-46 — **"The Proper RULES for FASTING!" (The Complete Instruction Manual for True Repentance!) By The Worldwide People's Revolution!®** Book 046, which is a

Companion Book of the above mentioned Book, which contains a True Life Story about an Old Black Mare called Lucy, who Fasted for 30 Days without Food nor Water, who was Physiologically "Born Again," as Jesus might say. See the Full Details in: **"The New MAGNIFIED Version of The GOOD NEWS According to Saint JOHN!" (The Gospel According to Saint John Zebedee Boanerges in Plain English!)** Book 062, which contains many Inspiring Photographs with Explanations!

[_] 21-47 — **"Are Americans the Most STUPID People who ever Lived?" (HOW Working People can PROSPER and Live in PEACE Under the Rulership of a RIGHTEOUS KING!) By The Worldwide People's Revolution!®** Book 047. (The Cover Photo shows a large Portion of the Author's Living Room Floor, which is worth 100,000$, which is just another Good Example of what you can also have, just for Loving and Obeying your Elected King!)

[_] 21-48 — **"An Amazing Collection of Wit and Wisdom!" (The Marvelous Tale of the Colorful Peacock from Angel Ridge, and the Strong Rope of Everlasting Hope!) By The Worldwide People's Revolution!®** Book 048. (The Cover Photo shows a Book Display, which will be Greatly Enhanced during the Future, when all 350+ Inspired Books are on Display in a Swanky Truth-brary, as Opposed to the Public LIE-brary.)

[_] 21-49 — **"Justifications for Capitalizations!" (WHY The Worldwide People's Revolution!® Defies the School of Fools by Capitalizing LOVE and HATE!)** Book 049.

[_] 21-50 — **"The END of CONFUSION!" (The Great CELEBRATION of the Magnificent Wedding of the Most Humble Honest Nations, and the Grand Year of JUBILEE!) By The Worldwide People's Revolution!®** Book 050. (Just Try to Visualize those **"Seven Great Swanky Armies of Voluntary Working Soldiers"** Marching through the Valley of Megiddo, being Dressed in their Colorful Robes, while the Band Plays *The Battle Hymn of the Republic,* and the Choirs Sing the Praises of the Great KING of Kings! What a Sight and Sound that will be, which will be Climaxed in **"The Great World TEMPLE of PEACE,"** when the Nations will get Married, along with our Elected King! Come one, come all to **"The Great Worldwide TELEVISED Court HEARING,"** by Means of your Wide Flat-screen TVs, whereby you might Learn WHY, WHEN and HOW!) †‡

[_] 21-51 — **"The Loathsome Burdens of the Independent Jackasses!" (A New Civilized Approach for Quietly Solving our Massive Problems!) By The Worldwide People's Revolution!®** Book 051. (Just Think about the Multitude of almost Worthless Meetings of the Minds, who Strained themselves to Think of Reasonable Solutions for our Massive Problems, who sometimes even Prayed to God for Help; but, the Solutions have been here for no less than 40 Years — Thanks to the Spirit of Inspiration from GOD!)

[_] 21-52 — **"Are we Tax Slaves of a Lower Order than those Lying Edomites!" (HOW to be Liberated from all Slavery, Worldwide!) By The Worldwide People's Revolution!®** Book 052. {This Inspired Book once had another Title and Author, which was not Acceptable by Amazon, which has now been Restored in all of its Glory, and is Published by more Trustworthy People, who are not Afraid of Controversies, nor of: **"The Swanky Sword of Divine Truths!" (The Most Powerful Weapon in the Whole Universe!) By The Worldwide People's Revolution!®** Book 067.}

[_] 21-53 — **"The Great False Economy is now DEBUNKED!" (Adolf Hitler had a much Better Economic System!) By The Worldwide People's Revolution!® Book 053.** (Trust me, Adolf was no Saint; but, during the Day of God's Judgment, he will be Justified, while his Anti-Christ Opponents will be Condemned: beCause they Refused to Attend a Worldwide Radio Debate with Adolf Hitler, whose Arguments will Stand Up during the Day of Judgment, which would have Prevented World War 2, and thus Saved the Lives of no less than 60 Million People! Likewise, we Tax Slaves must now Act more Wisely, and DEMAND **"The Great Worldwide TELEVISED Court HEARING,"** Book 041, whereby we might Save the World from that Dreadful Battle of Megiddo, called *Armageddon!* Yes, the Ball is now in YOUR Hands, my Potential Friend or Enemy, and you are now Responsible for it. Therefore, do not Shirk your Duty as a Free Citizen; but, Help us to Spread this Message far and wide, whereby the Masses of People will be Demanding The GWTCH, and thus Prevent another far more Dreadful and Hateful World WAR!)

[_] 21-54 — **"The UGLY Scarred Dishonest Face of Poor Old Miserable UNCLE SAM!" (A Memorial Day Legacy!) By The Worldwide People's Revolution!® Book 054.** {NOTE: This Inspired Book was also Suppressed by Amazon, who will be most Ashamed of themselves if they do not Un-suppress it during the Future: beCause it will also be Published by People of Greater Faith, who Know for a Fact that it is the TRUTH! Therefore, just be Patient.}

[_] 21-55 — **"The United States of the Whole World!" (A True Global Economy for the Masses of Working People!) By The Worldwide People's Revolution!® Book 055.** (This Inspired Book contains many Colored Photographs with Explanations. It is a Good Book to Publish in Foreign Nations, who are not so Blinded by their Pride, who can See the Mountain of Lies much Better at a Distance from them: beCause of not being a Part of the American Corruption.) †‡

[_] 21-56 — **"The New RIGHTEOUS One-World Government!" (HOW to Establish a Righteous One-World Government without Going to WAR!) By The Worldwide People's Revolution!® Book 056.** (This is a KEY Book, which everyone should Study Carefully and Prayerfully.)

[_] 21-57 — **"Those Ridiculous Contradictions within the Holy Bible!" (HOW to Read the Mutilated Bible with an Open Mind!) By The Worldwide People's Revolution!® Book 057.** (Many Professing "Christians" Falsely Claim that their so-called *"Holy Bibles"* do not Contain any Contradictions, being "the Infallible Inspired Word of the Living God," but, without the Capitalized Words, and without Explaining just WHY there are more than 200 Contradictory Versions of it! This Book Reveals how to Deal with those Biblical Problems, and come to Understand WHY God Allowed it to Happen for the Truth's Sake. Trust me, you have never Heard this Explanation before now.)

[_] 21-58 — **"The Divided States of United Lies!" (The so-called "United States of North America" in Disguise!) By The Worldwide People's Revolution!® Book 058.** {NOTE: This is perhaps the most Referred to Book among all of the Books by our Selected King; but, that does not Mean that it is his Best Book by any Means, which is Well Camouflaged: so that it will Survive the Test of Time, even if the others are BURNED by the Anti-Christ Followers of Satan, who are Possession Worshipers of the Worst Kind, who Seek to Justify American Lies, rather than Quickly

Confess them, and thus Escape from their Self-made Prison of Propagandish Lies! Just be Perfectly Honest, and you will have no Problem with any of our Literature.}

[_] 21-59 — **"The Complete SURVEYS of our VALUES!" (SURVEYS of Religious Spiritual Political Governmental Sexual Social Moral Economic Business Labor Habitual and Miscellaneous VALUES!) By The Worldwide People's Revolution!®** Book 059. {NOTE: According to our Selected King, every Potential Leader in the World must Fill Out and File those Surveys on the Internet for everyone to Study, whereby the Best People might be Elected by those Wise People who have also Filled Out the Complete Surveys of their own Values, whereby they will be Qualified to VOTE. Otherwise, they will not be Qualified to Vote, which will Eliminate a LOT of Wasted Money on Election Deceptions, while at the same Time it will Educate a lot of Ignorant People, who Desperately Need to Study that Inspired Book before Voting for another Dimwitcrat, Reprobate, or Independent Jackass!}

[_] 21-60 — **"HOW to Get our PRIORITIES in ORDER!" (The Glories of Democracy; and, Does DEMON-ocracy have its Priorities in Order?) By The Worldwide People's Revolution!®** Book 060. This Book will need to be Re-written by a Collective Group of Wise People, who will Contribute their True Life Stories during the Future, when they Wake Up and come to their Right Senses with the Prodigal Son of *Luke 15*. See:

[_] 21-61 — **"The New MAGIFIED Version of The GOOD NEWS According to Saint LUKE!" (The Magnified Gospel of Saint Luke in Plain English!)** Book 061, which is by Far the Best Version of that Gospel on the Earth, which has no Rivals at all among the other 200+ Versions. Guaranteed!

[_] 21-62 — **"The New MAGNIFIED Version of The GOOD NEWS According to Saint JOHN!" (The Gospel According to Saint John Zebedee Boanerges in Plain English!)** Book 062, which also has no Rivals among all of the other Versions: beCause this is no Translation of anything; but, it is the Inspired Words of the Living God, which were Revealed by the Holy Spirit, who has not Died.

[_] 21-63 — **"The New MAGNIFIED Version of the Book of ACTS!" (The Understandable Version of the Acts of the Apostles in Plain English!) By The Worldwide People's Revolution!®** Book 063. (This Inspired Book makes it Understandable WHY the Jews Hated the Apostles so much. You will have to Read it to Believe it.)

[_] 21-64 — **"The New MAGNIFIED Version of the PSALMS of King David!" (The Understandable Version of the Famous Psalms in Plain English!)** Book 064. You will be Amazed!

[_] 21-65 — **"A List of FAIR Swanky Wages!" (The Equitable Wage System!) By The Worldwide People's Revolution!®** Book 065. (All Hardworking People will LOVE this Good Book!)

[_] 21-66 — **"Beautiful Swanky PALACES!" (A New Concept in Living Habits — Swanky Palaces for Poor People!) By The Worldwide People's Revolution!®** Book 066. (You have no Idea what a "Swanky Palace" IS, unless you have read this Unique Book.)

[_] 21-67 — **"The Swanky Sword of Divine Truths!" (The Most Powerful Weapon in the Whole Universe!)** Book 067. (The very Reason that our Selected King has no Rivals is beCause of the Swanky Sword of Divine Truths, which no one can Defeat by any Means. Therefore, you Need to have it on your own Side, whereby no one can Defeat your Arguments! Be Strong, be Brave, have Faith and put on the Whole Armor of GOD!)

[_] 21-68 — **"Has your Life become Extremely Complicated?" (HOW to Live a SIMPLE Life!) By The Worldwide People's Revolution!®** Book 068. (Many People are not even Aware of just how Complicated their Lives are, until suddenly they are ready to Commit Suicide! It is Best to Prevent all such Evil Things, and this Book tells HOW.)

[_] 21-69 — **"The IDEAL Place to Live!" (HOW to Discover the Ideal Place to Live!)** Book 069.

[_] 21-70 — **"Our Elected King Who Speaks Out!" (It is High Time for some Sane Person to Get Control of this Insane World!) By The Worldwide People's Revolution!®** Book 070. (This Inspired Book contains a Special Speech that is Addressed to both Houses of the Congress in Washington. You will Love it, O Man of Greater Faith!)

[_] 21-71 — **"How GAY is GOD?" (Oh the Wonders of it all when it ALL Hangs Out!)** Book 071. (Do not Judge the Book, until you have Carefully "Red" all of it. You will be Surprised by the Truths!)

[_] 21-72 — **"LIGHTNING STRIKES Versus Lightning Bugs and Impotent Fireflies!" (A Memorial Photo Album of some Real American Heroes!) By The Worldwide People's Revolution!®** Book 072. (NOTE: This Book is Unique among all of the Books by our Selected King: beCause he did not get to Proof-read it before the Computer Crashed. It just Happened to be Saved on a Computer Chip before the Computer Crashed, and therefore it was Saved in PDF. But, the Corrections did not get made, which makes it a Special Collector's Item, which has more than 100 Colored Photos, which was what Caused the Crash.) †‡

[_] 21-73 — **"The BEST of CAPITALISM!" (Corrections for: "LIGHTNING STRIKES Versus Lightning Bugs and Impotent Fireflies!")** Book 073. (It is a completely new Book, except for those Corrections; and it is one of the Best Books in the World, which all Honest People will Love.)

[_] 21-74 — **"LIGHTNING STRIKES Versus Lightning Bugs!" (HOW you can Become Moderately RICH, without Telling any Lies nor Selling any Trash!) By The Worldwide People's Revolution!®** Book 074, which is the Perfection of all of the Lightning Striking Books, which is Recommended above all others for Mass Production: beCause it stands the Best Chance of being a Real Winner, just after this Book that you are now Reading, which has a Magnetizing Title!

[_] 21-75 — **"What are the Punishments for Dietary Sins?" (Have we Served ourselves Well at the Tables of our Lusts?)** Book 075. (This Book is too Controversial to be Published at this Time. Be very Patient until it is Available: beCause it is HOT!)

[_] 21-76 — **"What is WRong with those CRAZY CHRISTIANS?"** (A Self-Examination of **the Heart of the Body of Good Government!) By The Worldwide People's Revolution!**® Book 076.

[_] 21-77 — **"The Gospel According to our Elected King!"** (The Good News from the Most **Modern Perspective!)** Book 077. (This is perhaps the Best Book that you will Discover on Amazon, which contains the Famous Sermon that Jonah gave to the Ninevites, plus a very Special Sermon by Jesus Christ, himself!)

[_] 21-78 — **"The Root Cause for almost all Evils!"** (The Strange Things that People Say and **Do to Get more Money!)** Book 078. (This Book contains many Colored Photographs with Fascinating Explanations!)

[_] 21-79 — **"Orgimmick Gardening at its Best!"** (HOW to Grow Delicious Satisfying Foods **without a 10-Million-Dollar Investment!) By The Worldwide People's Revolution!**® Book 079. (This Book also contains many Colored Photographs with Wonderful Explanations!)

[_] 21-80 — **"Guaranteed Solutions!"** (HOW to Solve our Local and Global Problems in the **Most Rational Manner Possible!)** Book 080. (See the Description on Amazon: because they Offer a ONE-MILLION-DOLLAR REWARD to anyone who can Prove our Selected King's Solutions to be WRong or Unworkable! Can you Beat that? Do you have all such Guaranteed Solutions? Only our Selected King has those Solutions: beCause God Blest him with those Provable Solutions, which can be Proven in any Courtroom with Law and Order.)

[_] 21-81 — **"Mexicans are more Intelligent than Americans!"** (A Unique Challenge to all **Americans and Mexicans!) By The Worldwide People's Revolution!**® Book 081. {NOTE: The Remaining 275 Inspired Books by the Author of this Book may only be found in English, until we can get them Properly Translated into other Languages. Shame on you People who Killed him, who Broke his Heart with your Unbelief. May God have Mercy on your Poor Wretched Souls.} †‡

[_] 21-82 — **"¡Los Mexicanos son más Inteligentes que los Estadounidenses!"** (¡Un Desafío **Único para todos los Estadounidenses y Mexicanos!) By The Worldwide People's Revolution!**® Book 082. {NOTA: Aquí está el primer Libro en Español, que puede no ser Perfecto; pero, es Perfectamente lo Suficientemente Bueno para Iluminar las Mentes de quien lo Estudia.}

[_] 21-83 — **"Was Billy Graham Greatly Deceived?"** (Giving Honor to whom Honor is Due!) **By The Worldwide People's Revolution!**® Book 083. {NOTE: If you know a Grahamite, please Direct him or her to this Inspired Book, whereby he or she might be Converted to the Truths within it, and thus be Saved from Grahamite Perversions. Thank you.}

[_] 21-84 — **"The New MAGNIFIED Version of the Book of DEUTERONOMY!"** (The **Understandable Version of Deuteronomy in Plain English!)** Book 084. This is actually one of the Best Books within the entire Holy Bible, and also one of the Longest; but, do not allow that Fact to Deter you by any Means: beCause, "the Bigger Book is Normally a Better Book," which is True of a lot of Books, including all of the above Books: beCause it is the Nature of the Holy Spirit to get into Long-winded Sermons, you might say, which is WHY the Apostle Paul Preached until Midnight in the Book of Acts, until some Boy fell from a Window and Killed himself, whom the Apostle Paul Raised Up from the Dead and went on Preaching until the Dawn of the Day! {See: **"The New MAGNIFIED Version of the Book of ACTS"** for the Finest of Details, Book 063.}

[_] 21-85 — **"All of the Arguments are in Favor of our Selected King, who has Zero Challengers!" (Before you Attend another Election Deception, you should Carefully Study this Inspired Book with an Honest Open Mind!) By The Worldwide People's Revolution!®** Book 085.